GERMAN GIRL

A Child in Nazi Germany

By

Erika Bredt Zeigler

Edited by Carla Zeigler Holiday

I hope that you will enjoy reading my memoirs of the past!

Erika Zeigler

Copyright © 2009 by Erika Bredt Zeigler

The right of Erika Bredt Zeigler to be identified as the author of the work has been asserted by her in accordance with the Copyright, Designs and Patents Act 1988.

All rights reserved. No part of this publication may be reproduced, stored in a retrieval system, or transmitted, in any form or by any means without the prior written permission of the publisher or author, nor be otherwise be circulated in any form of binding or cover other than that in which it is published and without a similar condition being imposed on the subsequent purchaser.

ISBN 1442132361

Cover design by Jon Holiday, Image One Media, Fort Worth, Texas

Main locations in Germany where I spent my childhood:
Rheydt, Sadelkow, Haldensleben, and Emmering

Contents

	Preface and Acknowledgements	7
1	A Special Day	9
2	On the Home Front	12
3	Christmas	24
4	Dark Days	35
5	My Mutti	48
6	Work and Play	54
7	A Momentous Decision	62
8	The War in Rheydt	68
9	Tante Traudchen	79
10	Emmering	82
11	Beginnings and Endings	89
12	Survival	98
13	Adventures with Berti	107
14	Evacuation to Sadelkow	116
15	Living with the Hahns	121
16	Escape to the West	128
17	Moving to Bavaria	137
18	A New Home	147
19	A New Family	159
20	A New Life	166
	Epilog	178

Preface and Acknowledgements

GERMAN GIRL records events I experienced as a young girl in Germany during World War II and in the years that followed the end of the Nazi regime. Looking back on those years filled with so much horror and destruction, I remember moments of happiness, days when I lived the fun, carefree life every child should experience. I remember smiles and laughter, and acts of kindness that cut through the oppressive cloud weighing us down day after day. And the more I thought about that time, the more I remembered the details of those days. Once I sat down and began to write, it was as if I were stepping back in time and reliving it all.

I was inspired to write my story by reading a story similar to my own. I felt an obligation to pass on my story to my children and their children so that they too could understand the events that shaped my life.

I wanted my children to know the people from my past who touched me and were important to me, those who suffered and survived those hard times, and those who ultimately lost their lives to an evil empire. They have traveled with me through the years as ever-present companions—innocent men, women, and children, gone but never forgotten.

Erika Bredt Zeigler
March 2009

Erika, around the age of four
in 1939 Germany

1 ~ *A Special Day*

As I think back to my early childhood, the memories of the time before the war are few. I see snatches of family gatherings, faces, names, and half-formed pictures of long walks and warm meals, all jumbled up in the recesses of my mind. But every so often, a memory springs forth startlingly clear and vivid, as if it only happened yesterday. The events of one particular November day in 1937 are forever imprinted on my mind. I was not yet three years old.

The day was cold and crisp. The sun broke through the clouds and added a shimmer to the streets wet with melted snow. The brilliant blue of the sky, after weeks of overcast gray, declared this day to be very special. On this particular day, as I played quietly on the floor of her neat apartment, my neighbor Frau Dudek called to me with excitement in her voice. "Erika," she said. "Let's go for a walk. I have something special to show you." She quickly helped me with my coat, hat and mittens, and took me by the hand. We walked down the three flights of stairs and onto Kirchstrasse, a cobblestone street lined with houses and apartment buildings, many connected to each other. We walked down the street, past the coal and briquettes handler where we purchased our fuel each winter, past the beautiful Lutheran Church on the corner, and past the Rheydt-Geneicken train station. We continued down the next block, lined with large Chestnut trees, bare during the winter season but promising the lush green foliage it delivered every spring.

Frau Dudek held my hand tightly as we crossed several more streets, finally reaching our destination, a small house at the end of a crowded block. When we entered the home, I noticed that Frau Dudek's voice dropped to a whisper. "Right this way, Erika. Through this door." I entered a small bedroom at the back of the house and immediately noticed Mutti, my mother, sitting on the side of a bed. She was wearing a deep red two-piece knitted outfit. Her black hair was brushed away from her beautiful face. She was 22 years old.

Frau Dudek picked me up to see the bundle lying in a tiny white wooden crib beside the bed. Wrapped inside a white crocheted blanket was a tiny newborn baby. Mutti finally spoke, "Erika, this is your brother Wilfried." He waved one little fist in the air and squinted his eyes. His little head was bald except for the slightest trace of blonde fuzz. He looked just like Mutti. My mother looked down at Wilfried with love in her eyes as she tucked the blanket closer around his squirming body. I felt so proud to have a little brother.

My baby brother Wilfried and me

2 ~ *On the Home Front*

The city of Rheydt is situated in northwest Germany in the Ruhr Valley, also known as the Rhineland, on a major rail connection for central Europe. With its proximity to transportation, and the abundant natural resources of the area, Rheydt became a key industrial city for Germany. Prior to the war, the city manufactured items like cotton, wool, and other textiles, as well as shoes, cables, machinery, tools, electrical equipment, and printing supplies. During the war, Rheydt, and all of the Ruhr Valley became strategic bombing sites for the Allied forces because of the transportation lines and industrial resources.

The Lutheran church Oma Bredt attended in Rheydt

Besides manufacturing facilities and the main rail station, the Rheydt landscape is dotted with both Catholic and Lutheran churches. But it's the beautiful Schloss Rheydt, or Castle Rheydt, that draws attention. Complete with moat, this impressive palace stands majestically just outside the city, amid lush green lawns and striking landscaping. The beautiful renaissance style architecture reflects in the surrounding water.

North wing of Schloss Rheydt

Schloss Rheydt was originally constructed in the 12th century, and then extensively redesigned in the 15th century. It is one of the best preserved examples of renaissance architecture. Today, part of it has been opened to the public as a museum dedicated to the history of the castle and the city of Rheydt.

My parents were Peter and Nelly Bredt. Including my brother and me, the four of us lived on Kirchenstrasse on the third floor of an apartment building in the city of Rheydt, in northwest Germany. When my father was called away to military service, my mother and I shared the small apartment. My grandparents Bredt also lived in the same building in the apartment next to us. A total of six families lived in our four-story apartment building.

The first floor was occupied by Frau Wefers and her teenaged daughter Hilde. The husband and son had once lived there as well, but difficulties with the law had prompted them to go elsewhere. Frau Wefers did not allow her circumstances to bring her down, however; she was a hard-working woman who made ends meet through her sewing business.

The second floor was shared by two families: an elderly couple named Horsch lived in one half of the apartment, while their daughter Kaete, her common-law husband Fritz Palmer and their young son, resided in the other half. Fritz, the only young man in the building, suffered from tuberculosis. Most of

Rheydt's young men had been drafted in to the army, but Fritz's ailment exempted him from military service. He made a living from their apartment by making and repairing shoes. Their young son Gunther was just a little older than myself at the time—about six years old.

Herr and Frau Horsch also had an unmarried son, August, who had been drafted into the army in 1939. Occasionally, he was allowed to come home on leave to visit his family. I remember him as a nice-looking quiet young man. About a year after his last leave, his parents were notified that he had been killed in action.

Besides myself, my mother, and my grandparents, the third floor was also home to Frau Anna Dudek and her husband Stanislaus. Frau Dudek, an elderly woman and a very devout Catholic, sometimes watched over me when my parents or grandparents were not available. She and her husband had emigrated from Poland some years earlier. Herr Dudek owned an auto

Frau Anna Dudek

15

repair shop a few blocks away, behind the train station. Unlike his wife, Herr Dudek always appeared grumpy and never smiled. He had a temper and frequently fought with his wife. Frau Dudek, however, treated my family with kindness. Often she would bring me a bowl of grated carrots with a cup of hot milk, something I enjoyed immensely. She frequently took me to church with her, or invited me to accompany her as she ran errands. I loved going with her to the local nursery. She loved flowers and always had flower pots overflowing with beautiful blooms on the sill outside her window during the spring and summer months.

Oma Bredt

The fourth floor was more like an attic which had been divided into one large room and four smaller rooms along one wall. Each family—the Bredts, the Dudeks, the Wefers, and the Horschs—had use of one of the small rooms. Some used their room

16

for storage; my family used our room for a bedroom. Before Papa left for the war, it was my parents' bedroom. Later, Mutti and I shared the room. The large attic room had clotheslines strung up—on cold or rainy days, we would hang our laundry to dry here.

My grandparents Bredt subdivided their apartment with my parents after they were married. Oma Bredt was a nice lady, devoted to God and very religious. Slimly built, she stood about average height and always wore dark clothing. Her long wavy gray hair was braided and pulled up into a bun. She had recently had most of her teeth pulled, and relied on her new set of dentures. She looked very attractive with her new teeth, and every evening she removed them to soak them in a cleaning solution. Each morning, she left for work at a nearby linen factory.

My grandfather, Opa Bredt, was not a very tall man, stand-

Opa Bredt

ing about the same height as Oma. At one time, Opa Bredt owned a bookbinding and framing business with his brother, but Opa contract lead-poisoning from handling the inked pages and was forced to retire early. Like Oma, he had lost his teeth, but covered his toothless mouth with a large handlebar moustache. I remember he always wore a suit with a stiff white collar attached to his shirt. He loved smoking his pipe and reading the daily paper. While Oma worked at the linen factory, Opa handled the cooking and daily housework. In his spare time, he enjoyed long walks, walking stick in hand, to visit his only daughter, Martha, who lived about a mile and a half away. Sometimes he rode the streetcar or train to visit his brothers and sisters in the neighboring city of Moenchengladbach.

Opa and Oma Bredt in their garden.

My father's parents had given us our apartment to live in until something better should come along. It was very difficult finding a place to live, and waiting lists were long. We had one large room which combined both the kitchen and living room. Up a small flight of stairs directly under the slanted roof was our bedroom. After Mutti came home with baby Wilfried, my parents managed to get one of the other four attic rooms that was being used for storage to use for Wilfried's room. I was so excited to have a brother, even though his presence meant of lot of extra work. Daily, Mutti washed his cloth diapers by boiling them in water, then rinsing them in cold water, and hanging them outside on the clothesline to dry. On very cold days, we hung his diapers in the large attic room.

Down a flight of stairs was an old-fashioned toilet. The water tank hung near the ceiling from which an elongated porcelain handle on a long chain dangled. When I pulled on the handle, the water rushed down fast, and I knew if I was slow in getting off the bowl my behind would get wet. A wash sink with cold water was right outside the door.

I have few memories of my father. Prior to being drafted into the German army, my father worked as a bookkeeper at a neighborhood bank. Once drafted, he was stationed in France during the German occupation. Whenever Papa came home on leave from the army, our family went for long walks to the park and to see our beautiful Rheydter Castle. During warm weather, we traveled to "Bella Muehle," the city's public swimming pool located between Rheydt and Odenkirchen, about fifteen minutes away by streetcar. My brother and I had a great time in the children's section where the water was low.

Papa on the right at age 17

Mutti, Wilfried and me at the Bella Muehle.
Papa was home on leave and took this photo.

The time soon came when Papa returned to the war. The house became quiet again without the bustle of visiting family and exciting trips across town. Even though most of the men were gone and the streets were quiet, there was still plenty to attract my interest. Farmers passed through with their horses and wagons to deliver large packages and crates to the train station. The horse traffic made walking on our cobblestone streets a bit risky—the horses always managed to leave a little remembrance behind, though people working for the city were assigned to keep the streets clean.

Living across the street from the train station Rheydt Geneicken was never boring. I watched the serviceman light the gas lantern outside the station every evening. I also enjoyed watching people catch the train; sometimes they had to run if they were late.

Geneikener Bahnhof, Rheydt

The Bredt Family

Above: Oma Bredt, Papa, Tante Martha, and Opa Bredt.
Below left: Papa and me. Below right: Papa and Wilfried.

Above left: Papa (standing, left) and friends.
Above right: Opa and Oma Bredt with their daughter Martha.
Below: Mutti and me with Oma and Opa. You can see pictures of Hindenburg and Hitler on the wall behind us.

3 ~ *Christmas*

Whenever Christmas approached, Rheydt became a magical place. We had not yet experienced any direct contact with the war, so things outwardly appeared peaceful. Sometimes snow blanketed the beautiful countryside giving it a quiet tranquil feeling. Our beautiful castle, Schloss Rheydt, was decorated for the special holiday season. Its many windows glowed with the twinkle of candlelight.

I do not remember that we ever had a Christmas tree in our home. Our now three-room apartment was very small. Also, because we were at war, most families tried to save their money for necessities. I do remember that my grandparents had an advent wreath with four candles on. Starting the first week of December, we would light one candle. Each week, we'd light another candle until it was Christmas day.

Those families that did have a Christmas tree did not set it up until Christmas Eve. Frau Dudek always had a tree with candles and pretty decorations. Typically, the evening before we went to midnight mass at the Catholic Church, she invited us over for homemade cookies and a hot glass of Gluehwine, a special holiday wine. She lit the candles on the tree and we sang Christmas songs. Christmas day was spent with the family.

We spent the Christmas of 1939 at my grandparents' apartment. I had just turned five a couple of weeks earlier. Wilfried was an adorable chubby two-year-old boy, so cute and the joy of everyone. He was the only son of an only son, the one who would carry on our family name "Bredt." Papa, Mutti, Oma and Opa were so happy and proud to have him in our family. We nicknamed him "Manni." Sometimes I was allowed to take Manni for a walk down the street. As more and more young men went off to war, the streets were mostly empty, with almost no cars. Women, children, and older couples were the only people around.

2-year-old Wilfried "Manni"

For our Christmas celebration, my mother baked cake and cookies, filling my grandparents' apartment with a wonderful mouthwatering aroma. Wilfried and I were proud to show off our brand new identical sweaters which Mutti had knitted by unraveling two army sweaters. A beautiful shade of red, the sweaters were also hand-embroidered by Mutti.

Tante Martha

Soon, the rest of the family arrived. My father's sister Tante Martha and her husband Uncle Emil, soon to be drafted in the German army, brought their two daughters, nine-year-old Edith and eight-year-old Renate. It was time to take our family picture. The bulky equipment was quickly set up, people positioned, hair smoothed and children hushed. We waited in anticipation for the bright flash—we were not disappointed as the bright light gave way to black spots before our eyes. It was very exciting.

Above left: Renate, Erika, and Edith
Above right: Tante Martha and Mutti
Below: Tante Martha with my cousins Edith and Renate,
Oma and Opa with me, about age two

For Christmas, Mutti knitted and embroidered matching red sweaters for Wilfried and me. She found the yarn by unraveling two army sweaters.

During the excitement after the family portrait, Oma and Opa slipped out of the room, only to return a few minutes later with presents for all the grandchildren. We eagerly opened our gifts. I don't remember what Manni received, but each of us girls received a beautiful doll! I had wished for one for a long time. The dolls given to Edith and Renate were about twice as large as the doll I received. I wondered why, but assumed it was because I was the youngest granddaughter, just turned five years old a couple of weeks

My cousins Edith and Renate and I each received dolls for Christmas from Oma and Opa Bredt.

earlier. I held my doll tightly—now I had my own baby, just like Mutti had my baby brother.

Papa came home on leave briefly in the spring. I remember the day he came home, I was looking out of our apartment window and saw him walking on Kirchstrasse about a block from our home. He was wearing his backpack and carrying a children's table and two small chairs, a gift for my little brother Manni and me, brought home all the way from France. For Mutti, he brought a beautiful crystal bowl with wavy edges and intricate etching. It stood on three little legs and Mutti loved it. He also gave her several meters of soft brown cashmere fabric, from which Mutti sewed herself a very stylish coat with matching turban hat. His time with us was short. Soon, he returned to join his fellow soldiers in France.

Mutti wearing the coat and hat she made from the cashmere my father brought her.

The very first air raid I can remember happened in May, shortly after he returned to duty. Mutti, Manni and I were sound asleep in our attic bedroom when suddenly Mutti was awakened by the warning sirens at about three in the morning. She quickly woke up Manni and me, and rushed us downstairs to the cellar. Everyone else in the house was already there; we were the last to arrive. We could hear explosions in the distance and the building rumbled with each blast. I was very scared. Finally, the all clear signal was given and we returned to our beds, though I don't think many of the families slept the rest of the night.

Allied air raid over the Ruhr Valley

The following morning, we read in the news reports that both Rheydt and Moenchengladbach had suffered damage; several homes had been destroyed and four people in Moenchengladbach had died. During the rest of the month, we experienced several more attacks, followed by a period of relative quiet before another series of air raids would once again target our little city. Little did I know then that this was just a taste of much more to come. Mutti did her best to help us go on and live as normal a life as we could anyway.

The end of 1940 quickly approached. My sixth birthday was just around the corner and I had known what I wanted for weeks. In fact, I had been pestering my mother for the longest time to allow me to have my ears pierced. Each time I asked, she wouldn't give me an answer. Then, a few days before my birthday, Mutti took me to the jewelry store, and asked me if I would like to have my ears pierced. Delighted, I immediately said yes.

First we chose my new earrings—a pretty pair of gold dangling earrings that were heart-shaped coral with a tiny gold dot in the center. Though I knew the piercing might hurt a little, I eagerly sat in the chair and waited as the jeweler began the piercing. Before I knew it, my ears were pierced. Though sore for a few days, the discomfort was well worth it. I was so proud of my new earrings and frequently spent time admiring my new look in the mirror!

Soon it was Christmas time again. Manni had just turned three when Papa came home again on leave. In his arms he carried Christmas presents for Manni and me. We each received a beautiful doll house with tiny fragile wooden furniture, because whatever I had, Manni had to have too. I eagerly began arranging the furniture in my dollhouse, being very careful with the delicate pieces. As I was playing, I glanced at Manni playing with the little fragile furniture Papa had given him. He was so happy, his chubby face smiling brightly.

Suddenly we heard a loud scream for joy and saw Manni proudly proclaiming, "Manni did it!" There in front of him was the wooden furniture, now a pile of broken wooden bits. He had broken every little piece of furniture into small pieces. He was so

Wilfried "Manni" Bredt

happy that he managed to do this. Looking at his little face all lit up with joy as he announced "Manni did it!" nobody was able to get angry at him. He was the darling of the family.

The following day, we were surprised when Mutti's brother Joseph unexpectedly came home on leave. I had not seen him in quite a while. He had been drafted into the war at age nineteen. I could not keep my eyes off of my handsome uncle. He had only seen Manni one time previously, and commented on how much both of us had grown. He stayed until evening and then returned to Odenkirchen by train to spend time with his parents. A few days later he returned to his duty in the war. What a nice reunion we had with my favorite uncle!

Joseph Boeckem

4 ~ Dark Days

Another year passed and soon it was 1941, the year that would mark our lives with grief and despair. Manni became sick, very sick. He was diagnosed with pleurisy and pneumonia (Rippenfellentzuendung). The war had resulted in shortages of many items, including medical supplies. Because Mutti had to spend every waking minute caring for Manni, she had very little time for me. I stayed with relatives—sometimes with Tante Martha and her family, and sometimes with my grandparents Boeckem (my mother's parents) who lived in nearby Odenkirchen.

The doctor came often to our house. Sometimes, when the doctor was unable to make the trip, Manni was carried over to the doctor's office, or taken by bicycle. Since it was early 1941, it was very cold outside. His body was burning with a high fever which resulted in his having hallucinations. As time went by, and he failed to get better, he lost weight. His already small body became smaller still. His bones were easily visible beneath his skin. He grew weaker and weaker, unable to stand or sit up. Finally he became so weak that his body was put in a cast. His eyes appeared to grow larger, with dark purplish shadows around his eyelids. His once chubby face now looked hollow and skeletal.

When family members came to see him, Manni usually did not recognize them. His hallucinations led him to believe there were ghosts or demons in the room. This terrified him. My grandfather Bredt would sit with Manni in his room to calm his fears and help him through his terrible visions. Opa kept a broom by his side. As Manni pointed out the demons in the room, Opa would chase them away with the broom until Manni said they were gone. But they always came back again, and the process would continue. Manni grew weaker throughout the spring and warming weather. Then one sunny summer day, my sweet little brother whom I loved so dearly, took his last breath at the age of three-and-a-half years old.

The funeral took place on a nice summer day. Many relatives and friends attended the small burial. I remember lots of tears and flowers. Manni was buried in a beautiful white casket in the children's section among many other young children who died due to illness or were killed during air raids. We didn't realize that there were so many young children who had

lost their lives.

Mutti was inconsolable. Papa was notified right away, but he received the message much later. His outfit was on the move from France to the Russia front. Communication was difficult. He finally arrived home on emergency leave two weeks after the funeral.

Wilfried "Manni" Bredt, 1937-1941

It was a very sad time for all of us, especially for my Papa who had to go back to the war with no time left to mourn the death of his only son.

Mutti and I visited Manni's grave often. He had a beautiful headstone with an Angel looking down on him. The cemetery was located near our main train station in Rheydt. It took us about thirty minutes by street car and then about an additional ten minutes walking. The whole cemetery looked like a park, and was well taken care of. We passed by many other graves, most well maintained, with flowers placed in remembrance, but some were badly neglected. I wondered if their loved ones were not around anymore to take care of the graves, because they too had died in this horrible war.

I don't clearly remember how we said our goodbyes to Papa as he left to rejoin his regiment on the Russian front. The devastation the war was causing became more and more evident. Several young men in our neighborhood came back early, losing a leg or arm or both, but were lucky to be home again. Others died in battle. Often, the families did not receive the bodies for burial. They were casualties of war, and frequently buried swiftly in mass graves. During Papa's service in the war, Mutti received many letters from him, but they took a very long to arrive. She stored them all in metal sewing machine box, nicely bundled up.

As my seventh birthday approached in December of 1941, we anxiously awaited the arrival of the daily mail. Everyday we looked for a letter from Papa. Some time had passed since his last letter had arrived, but we knew that the mail was no longer dependable. Letters could arrive weeks after being written, or might never arrive at all. We also knew that Papa was fighting on the Russian front in bitterly cold conditions. The winter of December 1941 in Russia was one of the coldest recorded.

The last mail received from Papa had been to my grandparents at the end of November. He said very little, but I never will forget these words "only God can bring us back home." He had a lot of faith and he wished us a safe and blessed Christmas. December came. Talk of the Japanese attack on Pearl Harbor on December 7th was the focus of attention. The entry of the United States into the war concerned many people. When Germany officially declared war on the United States a few days later, many knew the worst was still ahead. My birthday came and went amid all the news of war.

Finally, Christmas arrived and we knew sooner or later there had to be a letter in the mail from Papa. Our neighbors had received mail, why hadn't we? Everyone was thinking the worst but hoping for the best. My grandma Bredt, a very religious person and devoted to God, prayed a lot and read the Bible which gave her comfort. Christmas day was very quiet. Mutti and I went to midnight mass; Oma went to her Lutheran church down the street. Opa did not attend church very often but he was a very good man and believed in God.

1941 became 1942 without any word from Papa. Weeks passed. Finally, on February 6th, Mutti received a letter in the mail. Dated January 3rd, 1942, and signed by Hauptfeldwebel der Einheit, Otto Hahne, the letter stated that Papa had been killed in action in Wyschneje-Bolischoje, about 35 kilometers south of Livry in Russia on December 6th, 1941, one day before the Japanese attacked Pearl Harbor. He was 34 years old. He never knew about the attack, or that Germany had declared war on the United States. Papa and many other soldiers who died on that day were all buried in a mass grave in Russia. It took exactly two months for the news of his death to reach us.

Located south of Kiev, this burial site was dedicated to the German soldiers killed on the Russia front in December 1941. My father may be buried here in one of the many unmarked graves.

Our family was devastated. Mutti had lost her husband after losing her beloved Manni just months earlier. My grandparents lost their only son. Oma aged a lot, but her strong faith in God kept her going. Opa was very quiet and smoked his pipe, but you could see in his eyes the great loss and sadness. The death of Papa didn't hit me as hard because I never had the chance to really know him. Most of my memories were of times spent with Mutti and Manni, but I cried because everyone else was crying. Little did we know then that within six months of Papa's death, our family would be split into two, changing Mutti's and my life forever.

> Otto Hahne   O.U., den 3. Januar 1942.
> Oberfeldwebel.
>
> Frau
> Petronella Bredt,
> Rheydt /Rhld.,
> Kirchstr. 3.
>
>   Sehr geehrte Frau Bredt !
>   Für unser Deutschland fand am 6.12.1941 bei Wyschneje-Bolischoje, ca. 30 km südl. Livny, Ihr Gatte den Heldentod.
>   Ich spreche Ihnen und Ihren Angehörigen zu diesem herben Verlust mein und der gesamten Kompanie tiefempfundenes Beileid aus.
>   Ihr Mann, der in der Kompanie als Maschinengewehrschütze eingeteilt war, hat sämtliche Gefechte der Kompanie mitgemacht. Er hat sich stets voll eingesetzt und wurde am 14.10.41 vom Divisionskommandeur für Tapferkeit vor dem Feinde mit dem E.K. II ausgezeichnet.
>   So wie er sich soldatisch auszeichnete und damit die Achtung seiner Vorgesetzten und Kameraden hatte, war er durch seine Kameradschaft bei allen Kompanieangehörigen beliebt.
>   Das persönliche Eigentum Ihres Gatten ist von der Komp. sichergestellt und wird Ihnen sobald wie möglich zugestellt.
>   Nehmen Sie nochmals, sehr geehrte Frau Bredt, mein und der Kompanie tiefes Mitempfinden entgegen.
>
>   Hahne
>   Hauptfeldwebel der Einheit 1016 E.

Notification of Papa's death on December 6th, 1941 in Russia

Peter Bredt, 1907-1941

Most of the photographs of my father in uniform were taken during the German occupation of France in 1939-40. Above, my father is the soldier on the right.

Above: My father Peter Bredt is in the third row,
first man on the left. Below, Peter Bredt
is riding the first bike on the left.

Peter Bredt, 1907-1941

This is the last known letter by my father written to his parents on November 29th, 1941. He was killed the following week on December 6th. My second cousin Elke found the letter in her mother Renate's paperwork after Renate passed away. Elke gave me the letter—the only surviving letter by my father. My father had written many letters to my mother while he was away, but at some point many years after the war, my mother destroyed them all. He writes in part,

"My dear Parents, all hopes for a Christmas leave seem to be gone. It looks like it is going to be cancelled. We have already accepted this bad news. We are always told 'Move forward towards the enemy.' It gets harder each day, but we can't get soft on them. We are 150 km away from Voronegh. After arrival we will seek our winter quarters. Right now it is pretty quiet, but we have to be on constant lookout for the enemy. They are in the same village as us, only on the other side. My dear Parents, everything will be all right. We must trust in the Lord. He is the Almighty Leader… Greetings from your son, Peter."

.

5 ~ My Mutti

The loss of both Manni and Papa left a gaping hole in our lives. The continuing war also impacted each day. The man who came to light the gas street lights had not appeared in weeks. The whole city was kept pitch dark at night time in order to make it harder for our enemies to recognize and bomb targets in our city.

Being a heavy industrial city and part of the Ruhr Valley, Rheydt was a prime target for bombing raids. Many official buildings were closed due to the lack of personnel to staff them. Medical offices were almost non-existent. Doctors were needed to help in the war effort, so non-military people had little recourse in the event of illness or injury. Due to the many restrictions placed on Jews at this time, and the rumors of worse things happening, many Jewish people left all their possessions behind when they went into hiding or were smuggled out of the country.

Some things remained the same. Every morning Mutti set the alarm clock for 6:30 AM to get up and get me ready for school. After Manni's death, we gave up the extra room on the fourth floor, so we were back to one bedroom again. Neither the bedroom nor hallway was heated, so I dressed quickly. Mutti started the coal stove in our combined living/kitchen area located one floor below our bedroom. It was slowly warming up in the kitchen by the time I was dressed and ready for breakfast.

I loved the aromas that filled the kitchen each morning. Mutti had already ground her "imitation coffee beans" in the coffee mill, placing the mill between her knees and grinding away as I had seen her do so often. For breakfast, I occasionally ate a bowl of hot oatmeal soup, but most of the time I settled for two slices of rye bread with a boiling hot cup of fresh milk. I loved to dip my dry bread into the hot milk; I thought it was so good.

After breakfast, Mutti made sure I brushed my teeth. I didn't enjoy brushing my teeth—our toothpaste consisted of a horrible powdery substance that tasted like baking soda. It left a bad taste in my mouth. Next, Mutti made sure that I put on my warm coat which she had made for me out of an army blanket. I took my leather backpack and walked to school, about fifteen to twenty minutes away.

After I left for school each day, Mutti had a full day's work before her. Even though she had difficulty recovering from the deaths of my brother and father, she did not allow herself to quit the things that needed to be done. She always kept her mind and body busy. This helped her cope with an almost unbearable situation.

An excellent housekeeper, Mutti began each day by taking out the ash drawer of our stove. She carried the heavy drawer down four flights of stairs to the outside trash can to dump the ashes. Then she started a new fire to keep the apartment warm, and to use for cooking or baking. Daily she polished the top of the stove until it shone like a mirror. Every Saturday, she filled buckets with water, carried them up the stairs to heat the water, then poured the hot water into the portable bathtub, then walked back down again to refill them. It took her about a half of an hour to get the tub filled with enough warm water for me to take a bath. After I was finished, she went through the entire process again for herself. Then she had to use the buckets once more to drain the bathtub into the toilet. Like most people at that time, we did not have the luxury of a built in bathtub. No matter what the weather, she kept to this schedule. Perhaps the repetition brought some sort of order to her life like school brought to mine.

In addition to being a great housekeeper, Mutti was an excellent cook, preparing delicious meals from very little. With many items rationed due to the war, Mutti could work wonders with very few ingredients. She also knew how to sew, knit, crochet and embroider. In my eyes, my mother could do everything. I greatly admired her and wanted to be like her.

Besides taking care of me and the household, Mutti also took in outside work to help make ends meet. She had a contract with one of the local factories to sew military uniforms. Pre-cut pieces were delivered to the house and Mutti meticulously sewed the pieces together, finishing a set amount every day.

My mother, Nelly Bredt

The following day the completed uniforms were picked up and new pieces were delivered. This work provided us with enough money to live on, but money bought very little during the war. Trading on the black market was a common occurrence. Over time, Mutti traded most of Papa's clothes on the black market for essentials. She also traded the beautiful leather satchel he brought back from France and his brand new Leika camera.

But despite her rigid schedule and strong work ethic, Mutti went through a very rough time after the death of Papa and Manni. She was young and beautiful and very sad. She often suffered from depression, mood swings and anger. Sometimes, she took out her frustration on me. I was very careful around Mutti at times, trying hard to please her, but my efforts didn't always work. One wrong word and she would hit me in the mouth. I recall many times when my mother both verbally and physically abused me. Repeatedly, she'd scream, "Why did Wilfried have to die while you are still here? I wish it had been you—I wish you had died instead!" I longed for love from my mother, but sometimes it simply wasn't there.

One day, I came home from school and found Mutti extremely down. Though she never gave me the details, but I gathered that somebody had cheated her out of a lot of money. To have her hard work and ingenuity rewarded in this way, during an already difficult time after losing half her family and dealing with the deprivations of war, Mutti succumbed to a deep depression. I remember watching her turn on our portable double-burner gas stove without lighting the fire. I recall the smell of the gas as it floated across the room. I must have passed out because I don't know what happened after that. Maybe my grandparents or Frau Dudek came over and turned off the gas. Maybe Mutti had a change of heart and turned it off herself. Neither Mutti nor anyone else would ever talk about this matter afterwards. Thank God we survived.

On another occasion shortly after the stove incident, I came home from school early one afternoon to find blood all over the kitchen and on the ceiling. Mutti sat in a chair with her left wrist bandaged up. She told me she had been washing dishes and one of the bowls slipped out of her hands, broke, and slashed her wrist. The glass had cut an artery, and the blood had shot straight up to the ceiling. A doctor had come over to bandage the wound. She assured me not to worry because it was an accident and that she would be more careful in the future. I wondered, was it really an accident? Anyway, the rest of her life she carried a nasty scar on her wrist.

6 ~ Work and Play

Every day on my way to school I passed the birthplace of Dr. Josef Goebbels, Hitler's Propaganda Minister. On certain German holidays, like Mayfest, Adolf Hitler our Fuehrer visited the city of Rheydt. I remember one occasion in particular when the entire city was decorated with flags. Thousands of people and their children gathered at the Market Place to hear him speak. From a distance, I saw the Fuehrer shaking hands with many adults and children. Unfortunately, Mutti and I were too far away for contact.

In the spring of 1942, I moved into the second grade of elementary school. School began promptly at eight every morning, six days a week, and ended at one o'clock. We had one break in the morning during which we usually played outside. A second break was allowed for eating a snack brought from home.

My teacher, Fraulein Gertrud Kloeckner, was an elderly woman in her upper 60s or early 70s. Though very strict, she was well liked and respected by the

Hitler and Goebbels often visited Rheydt, Goebbels' hometown, drawing huge crowds.

Goebbels attended school here from 1909 to 1917 in Rheydt

students. She and her sister were both unmarried, having devoted their whole lives to teaching. Occasionally, my friends and I would see Fraulein Kloeckner walking to school in the morning along our same route. Whenever this happened, we each hoped for the honor of carrying her brown leather briefcase. It meant a lot to us to have this little bit of recognition in our lives.

Every morning after row call, Fraulein Kloeckner had us stand at attention before the huge portrait of Adolf Hitler that covered much of one wall in our classroom. We were required to swear allegiance to the Fuehrer and sing a military song. Then our daily routine began.

First, we had our fingernails inspected to make sure they were short and clean. Each of us students had our own chalkboard wiper attached by a string to our writing board—this too was checked daily for cleanliness. Next, each student was examined for

My 2nd grade class picture taken in 1942 at Wilhelm-Strauss School in Rheydt. I am sitting down just right of center. This school was bombed during an air raid in 1943.

head lice. Two students in our class had repeated problems with lice. One girl was the daughter of a Gypsy family from Hungaria (Ungarn) who had settled temporarily in Germany. The other girl named Ilse came from a poor family with many children. I sat behind her in class and often saw lice on her collar. We had to report her but I felt so sorry for her because it happened over and over again. When lice were detected, that student's parents were notified and the student went home. After this we were ready to begin the school day.

I was a pretty good student, except when it came to memorizing. I had to work harder than the other students to store information, but I refused to give up. I've often wondered why this is so. Several different events may have contributed to this condition. When I was a six-month-old baby, I was sitting on the kitchen table when Mutti stepped away for just a moment. I fell from the table, cutting the back of my head and my bottom. Blood gushed from both wounds as I screamed. My mother held me and took care of my wounds. I recovered, seemingly back to normal. Then, a few years later, I slipped and fell down the steep set of concrete stairs that led to our outside wash house. I received a terrible blow to my head. Mutti took me to the hospital where it was discovered that I had suffered a concussion.

By the time I was five years old, I began suffering from severe pounding headaches. Homework, especially memory work, made the headaches worse. I don't know if these prior injuries had any connection to my recurring headaches. Both my parents had headaches; Papa especially suffered with migraines. Whether inherited, or a result of my childhood accidents, my headaches were so severe they often made me sick. Mutti took me to several doctors specializing in headaches, but as a five-year-old girl, my complaints were not generally taken seriously. One doctor said I was too young to have so many severe headaches.

Headache or not, I persevered in school and tried to do my best. I enjoyed the structure and orderliness that school offered in a world that was largely chaotic and unpredictable. Though my memory problems forced me to work that much harder in the classroom, school was still a welcome retreat from the sadness and stress that seemed to fill the rest of my day. After school, I walked home and changed out of my school clothes. Dinner (Mittagessen) was always waiting for me, and then homework. Sometimes there was a lot of homework, especially when I had to miss school due to air raids.

When I wasn't in school, I either played with my friends or playacted by myself. Particularly on rainy days, I enjoyed acting out different stories for entertainment. Like many children my age, I enjoyed playing "store." The perfect place for playing store was on the stairs leading up to the fourth floor of our apartment building where I pretty much didn't have to worry about being in anyone's way. After setting up my store, I sent out little invitations to the other tenants living in the apartment. I used buttons and pennies for money. I had so much fun, especially when the tenants came to "buy" my wares.

Other times I pretended to be a seamstress like Mutti. I was not allowed to use the sewing machine, so all my work was done by hand. Mutti would give me leftover fabric remnants from which I created lots of doll clothes like dresses, skirts, blouses, coats and even underwear. After creating my little treasures, I would take the clothing to my friends Hildegard and Marlene and we would trade. In this way, I was able to have things I would otherwise have no way of getting. I remember coming home one time with a cut-out paper doll with a set of paper clothes.

On other occasions, I traded my doll clothes for "Glanzbilder." These were beautiful glossy cut-out pictures of things like flower bouquets, angels, children and animals. They came in many shapes, colors and sizes. I began a collection of Glanzbilder, saving the pieces in a praline box Mutti had kept from better times. Sometimes Mutti added additional bilder from the Woolworth store to increase my collection. Whenever I had duplicate pieces, I would trade with my girlfriends—we each had our own Glanzbilder collection!

7 ~ A Momentous Decision

Spring turned into summer and things began looking up again. Mutti had an opportunity to receive training for a great job as a "Nachrichtenhelferin," helping with war correspondence. However, in order to receive the training, she would need to find a place for me to live full-time. She had heard about a Catholic home that took in orphans and the children of women working for Hitler. This home was located in Allgau, deep in South Germany. Since the deaths of Manni and Papa, I was very fearful of losing Mutti as well. She was all I had left in this world and the last person on earth I wanted to be parted from.

Knowing that any separation would be very traumatic for me, and most likely bring about a flood of tears, Mutti chose to not fully communicate what I could expect to happen once we reached Allgau. The day for the trip arrived. To reach Allgau meant a long trip by train. Our luggage was packed and we left very early in the morning to begin our journey. First we took the street car to get to the main train station. There we waited for a long time.

Finally our "Schnellzug" or fast train arrived. The train was composed of old, pre-World War I carriages. Mutti had purchased tickets in the third-class compartment. Seating consisted of hard wooden benches. Every compartment was accessed through its own outside door, leaving little space for walking around between the two facing benches. People quickly showed their annoyance with us when we tried to walk from one side of the carriage to the other, stumbling over their feet.

The train was packed with soldiers, civilians and children. For a while, Mutti and I had to stand until some seated passengers arrived at their destination and vacated their seats. Once seated on the hard bench, Mutti quickly fell into a deep sleep amid all the noise and bustle within the train compartment, and the uncomfortable seating. She was exhausted, having slept little in the nights prior to our trip. I was seated next to a window. I stared out at the beautiful Rhine River, and gazed in amazement at the majestic double-towered cathedral as we passed through Cologne. As the cityscape gave way once more to countryside, I marveled at the glorious mountains along the river, dotted with castles from other mysterious lifetimes. I thought about who might have once lived there and was swept up in daydreams of kings and queens, knights and damsels in distress. But then the train would pass by a town or village scarred and broken by recent air raids, homes now piles of rubble, families sitting without hope in the bits and pieces that were now their lives. And my dreams of other worlds and faraway places were quickly shattered by the harsh reality of war. The contrast was astounding. So much beauty followed by so much despair.

Numerous castles dot the landscape along the Rhine River

After a while, Mutti finally awoke and prepared our lunch. She had packed sandwiches, fruit and lemonade before leaving home. As we ate, the train stopped often, taking on more and more passengers. All the seats were taken; many people were standing. After some time, the trend reversed itself and the train began to take on fewer passengers and release more.

At one point, the space beside Mutti became available and a soldier sat down, striking up a conversation with my mother. I heard my mother tell him about her job training opportunity and the reason for our trip to Allgau. The soldier encouraged my mother to work for the Fuehrer and the Third Reich. He said she was doing the right thing. As the conversation continued, I felt a sick knot develop in my stomach as fear of losing Mutti became more real. Nobody understood how lonesome and alone I felt. I also felt great dislike for the soldier for trying to persuade my mother to do the very thing that I feared the most. Thankfully, their conversation ended as the approaching evening darkened the train compartment.

Late in the evening the train slowed to a stop in Allgau. We made our way toward the door, luggage in hand. I don't remember what city or town we were in, but we quickly found a hotel. With all the stress of the journey and my own anxieties about what might lie ahead, we silently prepared for bed. As I allowed my mind to become consumed with worry over being separated from my mother, Mutti was dealing with her own guilt feelings about leaving me with strangers so far from the only home I had ever known. Needless to say, neither of us slept much that night.

Early that morning we walked to the orphanage. The large formidable building looked like a prison to me. We passed through the massive oak doors with heavy iron fittings into a dimly lit hall. Two nuns in black habits approached my mother and greeted her in words I couldn't understand. Their dialect was so completely different from ours, it sounded foreign to me.

My anxiety level rose as my heart began racing; I honestly thought I would faint dead away right there. Miraculously, I remained standing as one of the nuns introduced us to a few of the resident children. Most of them were orphans, having lost both their parents in the war. Next the nun escorted my mother and me around the premises. Everything looked strange and different. Finally, she showed us the room that I would be staying in. It was a large community room lined with beds. I would be sleeping with many other children. The nun then left Mutti and me alone.

Any fortitude I had shown up to that point was now gone. Tears rolled down my face as I begged Mutti not to leave me here. She tried to reassure me, telling me it would not be for long, but I was inconsolable. We returned to the hotel to talk some more. I don't know if it was compassion, guilt, or a little of both that finally motivated Mutti to change her mind. My happiness was beyond words. Mutti chose me and not the job. I was more important to Mutti than a well-paying job. I was ecstatic.

First thing the next morning we were on the train again beginning the long trip back home. My heart was light as I sat beside my mother. During the trip, I walked back and forth down the train aisle saying hello to everyone I saw. I wanted everyone to share my joy. The only dark spot in an otherwise glorious day occurred when I went to use the toilet on the train. I accidentally slammed the tips of my fingers in the door. I ran back to Mutti screaming, holding up my swollen fingers, now pounding with pain. I don't know what Mutti did to ease the pain, but anything felt better than staying behind in Allgau.

8 ~ *The War in Rheydt*

It was a very cold winter morning with little sleep in our attic bedroom. Next to the bedroom, we kept our large portable tub filled with water. The Civil Defense had ordered all citizens to do so. If the stairs should catch fire during a fire bomb attack, the water could be used to put out the fire and allow us to escape safely to the cellar or out of the building without being trapped. This night, the warning sirens went off again around 2:00 a.m., the usual time. We quickly got ready, throwing on several layers of clothing and running down four flights of stairs to the cellar. We were usually the last to arrive. The bombing of our city had begun.

The air raid sirens sounded almost every night. Each time we huddled in the cellar for about an hour until another siren alerted us that everything was clear. Then Mutti and I would climb the four flights of stairs through the cold house and try to go back to sleep. I fell asleep quickly. The sound of the sirens and the march up and down the stairs became routine, like brushing your teeth. I never felt worried because I knew Mutti would take care of me. Mutti, however, slept little. She knew the air raid siren could sound again the same night, and the process would begin again.

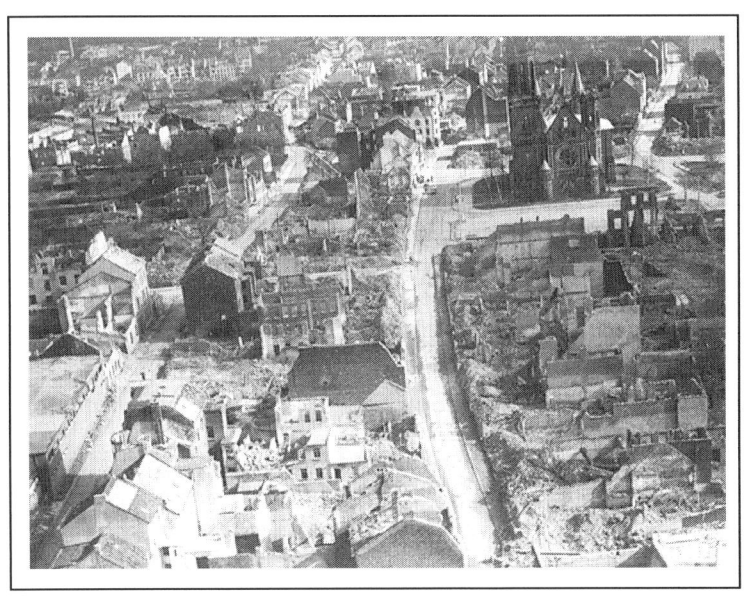

After weeks of air raids, many of Rheydt's buildings were utterly destroyed.

The nightly black-outs and air raid sirens were not the only signs of war that darkened our lives. People began to mysteriously vanish. I remember in particular a very nice couple who lived in the building beside ours. They worked at the nearby Cablewerk factory. Every day, they rode their bikes to work. At five o'clock they returned home. I did not have a bike of my own, so I used to wait for them to come home from work. The man Julius would frequently stop and allow me to get on his bike. He taught me how to maintain my balance and pedal. I looked forward to seeing him everyday.

I noticed that Julius and his wife began wearing a yellow star on their clothing. My mother told me that the yellow star was a sign that every Jewish person had to wear by order of Adolph Hitler the Fuehrer. I didn't think much of it at the time; I still waited eagerly every day for my chance to ride a bike!

One afternoon, I waited for Julius but he didn't come. I returned the next day, but still he didn't come. For several days I looked for him and his wife, but I never saw them again. I asked my mother where they had gone. She said they may have decided to leave the country. Many people—not only Jews—were finding ways to leave Germany. She also told me what the newspapers said—all Jews were being returned to their homeland of Palestine. I accepted what she said. I knew that curiosity and asking questions brought trouble to people. As time went by, I saw fewer and few of the yellow stars.

There were many rumors about where the Jews might really be going, but no one knew for certain. Also, people had to be very careful what they said aloud. Everyone knew Hitler had spies living among the townspeople. It was not uncommon for non-Jews to be arrested or simply vanish after having spoken to the wrong people about the wrong things. I heard about a minister of a local congregation who spoke out against Hitler in one of his sermons. The following week, he and his family vanished. No one knew if they had escaped or been arrested. And no one wanted to talk about it for fear of what might happen to them.

In the building on the other side of Julius' building lived Frau Hoffman, a widower, and her son Arthur, a friend of mine. Arthur's mother served as a volunteer to the Nazi party. She wore a Hackenkreuz (swastika) pin as a sign of her allegiance. It was her job to make sure that all the windows in the neighborhood were properly darkened at night so the enemy, flying overhead, would not be able to identify the location of the cities with their train stations and factories. Frau Hoffmann walked nearly every evening through the streets to check for light. I remember watching her stand closely against the buildings looking straight up for a glimpse of light shining through the cracks. Every small crack of light was reported to the Nazis. The consequences of not following the rules were severe. Interestingly, like so many of the volunteers, Frau Hoffmann faithfully attended the Catholic Church. Whenever she entered the church, she took off her Hackenkreuz pin. On the way home she promptly attached her pin again.

The Marienplatz in Rheydt—where Mutti and I caught the streetcar

One Saturday we went to visit my Grandma and Grandpa Boeckem in Odenkirchen, as we often did. I did not call my mother's parents "Oma" and "Opa" like I did my father's parents. Rather, I called them the same thing Mutti called them, "Mutter" and "Vater." We caught the streetcar a few minutes away from our house. The trip lasted about forty-five minutes and involved many stops along the way. In downtown Rheydt, we switched streetcars at the Marienplatz, next to the Marienkirche. The Marienkirche was the largest Catholic Church in Rheydt. Mutti and I attended mass there every Sunday. Finally, we arrived in the town of Odenkirchen.

My mother's parents: Joseph and Nelly Boeckem

We walked the remainder of the way to the home of Mutti's parents. Their home was situated across the street from the Niers, a filthy rat-infested river. My grandparents' home was built in the late 1800s, a gray two-story building with crumbling plaster walls and windows at almost sidewalk level because the main floor was below ground level. A step-down entry led to a narrow unlit hallway with a low ceiling.

The floorboards creaked with age. The home had no electricity; instead, a ceiling-mounted gas lamp was activated by pulling one of two strings. Running cold water was in the downstairs hallway, the only water supply available in the house. A toilet was located outside beside the pig stall.

Grandpa Boeckem raised two pigs on the property, as well as rabbits and chickens. His backyard was filled with fruit trees and every kind of berry bush. The scent of many flowers thickened the air with perfume. Grandpa Boeckem kept a second garden of vegetables and more fruit trees about two blocks away.

On this particular day, I rang the hand-operated door bell. Grandma Boeckem opened the door, her face lit up with her usual smile. Her long graying hair was pulled back in a bun. Her hands showed the effects of years of hard work. She wore a simple linen dress with an apron which covered her big bosom down to the hem of her dress.

Whenever Mutti and I came to visit, Grandma Boeckem walked to the bakery down the street and bought pastries. We drank "Ersatz Kaffee" (not real coffee) and treated ourselves with a choice of pastry or cake at the traditional four o'clock time. On this visit, we planned to stay overnight in one of the smaller upper floor bedrooms with creaky floorboards. I loved visiting my mother's parents, but I hated using the outhouse. It smelled awful. Being so close to the Niers River, I had to watch out for rats in the outhouse, especially at night.

The following morning was Sunday. After a wonderful breakfast of crispy hot rolls (Broetchen) with jelly or jam, sandwich meat, cheese, boiled eggs, coffee and hot milk, we all left for mass at the main Catholic Church in downtown Odenkirchen. After mass, we stopped by Grandpa Boeckem's big garden around the corner. It was a beautiful day without air raids. I ate fruit from the trees and large sweet strawberries straight off the plant. I also had a great time playing with Berti. Officially, though only two and a half years older than me, Berti was my uncle, since he

My "uncle" Berti on the right with Mutti and Tante Gertrud. I am on the far left.

was Mutti's younger brother. Berti was born late in my grandparents' lives. He had many toys in the garden shed—many more than I owned—and I had a wonderful day playing, just like a normal child.

As the time approached for us to leave, Grandma Boeckem packed up fruit and vegetables for us to take home. We said our goodbyes and left by train. We arrived in half the time it took the streetcar to arrive. I recall that weekend as one of the nicer times spent with my grandparents. It almost seemed like there was no war.

Berti on the left, Mutti holding Manni, Tante Gertrud, and my grandfather Boeckem (whom I called "Vater")

Some of our visits to the home of Mutti's parents were not as pleasant as this one. Mutti's papa had a terrible temper and certain things would set him off. Mutti and he often clashed. One day I will never forget. While visiting her parents on one particular Sunday, the family went to mass at the local Catholic

The Boeckem Family

Above:
My grandparents Boeckem with Berti, their youngest son

Right:
The older Boeckem children, Nelly, Gertrud, and Joseph (from right to left)

Church. Mutti had worn her high heels. When she came back to the house, she took them off because her feet were hurting. The family sat in the living room talking while I played outside with the gray striped cat Mitzi. Suddenly my attention was grabbed when the nice quiet conversation inside changed abruptly into yelling and screaming. I ran in the house in time to see my grandfather beating Mutti with her one of her high heels. Terrified, I began crying. My grandma did not say one word and continued on what she was doing. Our visit on that occasion turned out to be shorter than usual.

9 ~ *Tante Traudchen*

Mutti had other family members living near by as well. Occasionally, we visited my great aunt "Tante" Traudchen Dresen, the youngest sister of my Grandma Boeckem. By train it took us about thirty minutes to arrive at her home in a village called Jackerath. The train stopped in every little village on the way. Tante Traudchen lived in a much safer neighborhood than we did. She owned a small house with a very large garden. She was about fifteen years older than Mutti yet lived alone. One bad experience had changed her life forever.

When Tante Traudchen was young, she was also very beautiful. She fell in love and planned to marry a young German man. The First World War intervened, and her young man was drafted into the army. They planned to marry as soon as the War was over. She wrote to him often, and treasured every letter he sent by return mail. Everyone in the small village knew her and the deep love she had for her soldier.

As the end of the War approached, Tante Traudchen became uneasy. She so looked forward to seeing the love of her life soon. Then one night she had a fitful sleep. She dreamed that she was standing at the window of her own house, looking out at the front yard. The mailman walked up to her and handed her a telegram, saying, "Traudchen, I have bad news…" The dream bothered her deeply. She could not shake the ominous feeling the dream had left with her.

A few days later she stood looking out her window, and saw the mailman approach. She felt a knot form in her stomach. Mechanically, she opened the front door and stared at the compassionate face of the mailman. She listened to the words she already knew in her heart, "Traudchen, I have bad news." Her fiancé had been killed in the final days of the war. From that moment on, something snapped in her brain and she began talking to herself and acting as if her soldier were right there with her.

On this particular day, we knocked on her door. She answered with a huge smile—she was always happy to see us and made us feel very welcome in her neat and comfortable home. She was in her mid-forties, but to me she seemed much older. As usual, she took us to her beautiful vegetable garden. She grew all her own vegetables here. The garden was surrounded with fruit trees, and lots of raspberry, gooseberry and currant berry bushes. In bright pockets here and there, beautiful flower mounds of differing sizes added to the already dizzying array of scents and colors. That night, she prepared a delicious meal for us. No one cooked better then Tante Traudchen, not even Mutti. A wide variety of tasty vegetables and fruit were served with the meal. We stayed overnight like we did so often and left the next afternoon.

Tante Traudchen never got over the loss of her fiancé. When she was with us, she acted almost normal. Her voice was a bit shaky at times and occasionally she mumbled her words, but those things were minor. However, the moment we left her alone, whether we went outside or simply to an adjoining room, we could hear her talking either to herself or to someone not present.

Only her strong faith in God kept her going. Many years after I had grown and moved away, I heard news that she had died alone while sleeping. I like to imagine that she woke up in the arms of the fiancé she had lost so many years before. The whole village turned out for her funeral. She was well loved.

10 ~ Emmering

One day, Mutti and I planned another trip to visit relatives. This time we were going to see Mutti's only sister, Tante Gertrud. She had recently married a German pilot from the Luftwaffe air force. Onkel Hans and Tante Gertrud were transferred to the German air base at Fuerstenfeldbruck in Oberbayern or Bavaria. They were renting a small house in Emmering close to the air base. We planned on staying for several weeks while school was on break.

Mutti had never met Tante Gertrud's new husband, so she and I took the long train trip to Southern Germany once more. Traveling took all day long. We spent many hours along the Rhine River with its pictur-

Tante Gertrud

esque (Sieben Gebirge) mountains and romantic castles. The train was an express and stopped only in big cities. We arrived in Munich that evening and transferred to a train heading for Fuerstenfeldbruck, about forty minutes away.

The southern part of Germany did not experience the onslaught of regular air raids that we experienced in Rheydt. Because this part of the country did not have the number of factories or manufacturing plants that the Ruhr Valley had, it was not as strategic a target during the war. To me, not having air raids made it seem like the war was temporarily over.

When we got off the train at Fuerstenfeldbruck, my aunt was waiting to greet us. Tante Gertrud looked as pretty as ever with the dark brown hair and eyes that also characterized Grandma Boeckem in her younger days. Mutti, two years older than Tante Gertrud, had acquired the black curly hair and blue eyes of her father.

Mutti and little sister Gertrud

After hugs and greetings, the three of us walked the remaining mile and a half with our luggage to Emmering. By the time we saw the house on the horizon, I was dead tired. It was very late in the evening. I barely managed to eat a bite before I was shuffled off to bed. Onkel Hans was away on a flying mission until the following day, so Mutti and Tante Gertrud stayed up talking until late in the night, catching up on all that had happened since they last saw each other.

The following day, Onkel Hans returned home. I was very proud to meet him and be his niece. He looked very sharp and handsome in his pilot uniform. Tante Gertrud also introduced Mutti and me to her next door neighbor Frau Toni Zillner. Frau Zillner was about fifteen years older than Mutti, and had lots of wrinkles. She had lost her husband and lived in a two story home with her two sons Ludwig and Erich, and her daughter Helene.

Onkel Hans with Berti and me on a visit to Odenkirchen, 1943

Ludwig, or Wig, was the eldest and was only home temporarily while on military leave. Erich was twelve at the time and Helene was eight, only one year older than me.

Erich, Helene and I became good friends. Sometimes I had difficulty understanding them because of their heavy southern accent, but we managed to communicate enough to get along well. Strangely enough, Helene taught me how to walk barefoot. I had never done such a thing before—no one walked barefoot in the city. It was not as easy as it looked. More than once I stumbled and bloodied my big toe! Sometimes Helene and I would walk to the nearby Amper River. It was a clean river with several branches that meandered through the village. Even though I didn't know how to swim, I had so much fun. Frequently we played in the Zillner's backyard, doing such wonderful childhood games like hide and seek and jump rope. I loved every minute of it.

My friend Helene Zillner

My aunt and uncle only had one bedroom in their small home, so Frau Zillner asked my mother and me if we would like to stay with her in her extra room. We were happy to accept her offer. After our first night in the Zillner house, we were rudely awakened at 5:00 a.m. by an incredibly loud rooster! As a "city girl," I was not used to this daily early morning alarm.

Shortly after our arrival, Frau Zillner's 25-year old son began to take an interest in Mutti. Even though she was a few years older than him, they spent a lot of time together. I would hear them giggling and laughing quite a bit after I went to bed. However, their relationship never developed into anything more because Wig's leave was soon over and he had to return to the front. (Several months later, after we had returned to Rheydt, we received the tragic news that Wig had been killed in action. This was a big shock to Mutti and very sad news for the Zillner family.)

School break was officially over, but Mutti was not ready to return home. She decided that we would stay a bit longer in Emmering. She enrolled me in the local school. My new teacher's name was Fraulein Scharls, a friendly woman who was much younger than my teacher back in Rheydt. By this time I had met several of Helene's friends, and now I made more new friends at school, though some of the students made fun of my accent.

I remember one weekend trip in particular. We and the Zillners took the bus to a place called Dachau, about ten miles from Emmering. Frau Zillner's sister and her family lived there. While visiting, we had to walk past a heavily guarded prison camp on several

The main gates at Dachau after the liberation in 1945

occasions. When I asked about it, I was told that it was a "bad place." Nobody would say what happened there. Either they didn't know or they were afraid to say. People were not permitted to ask questions about prisoners or camps. If you displayed too much interest or curiosity, you could get into serious trouble. After the war ended, I learned that Dachau's prison camp was responsible for the death of thousands of Jews, handicapped people, political prisoners and Christian religious prisoners.

Eventually, our stay in Emmering came to an end. I had to say goodbye to my new school friends and teacher, to Tante Gertrud and Onkel Hans, to the Zillner family: Erich and Helene. We promised to keep in touch. Early the next morning Mutti and I boarded a train back home. By late evening, we were back in Rheydt once again.

11 ~ *Beginnings and Endings*

1942 came to an end, marked with both highs and lows. Though 1943 brought with it the hope that things would get better, reality presented a different story. I had turned eight years old in December, and already much had happened in my life that few adults have experienced. But still I try to look at the few events that brought a moment of joy or day of peace to our otherwise bleak existence.

1943 was the last year that our milkman made his daily visits to the house. During 1943, air raids no longer happened only at night. At any moment the sound of the sirens could pierce the air, sending everyone in search of cover. But 1943 also brought about the birth of Tante Gertrud and Onkel Hans' first child, a son they named Ingo. I so looked forward to meeting my new cousin when we next had the chance to visit Emmering. And 1943 marked the time of my First Communion, a major event in the life of any Catholic.

My First Communion was scheduled for Sunday, April 25th, and required weeks of preparation. Many boys and girls were expected to participate. All the girls had to wear white dresses. Since dresses were not available in stores at this point during the war, everyone had to find a way to make their own. I was lucky that I had a mother who know how to do just about everything, I admired her so much and I knew already then that when I grew up I would try to be just like her. Mutti had spent hours of time sewing my beautiful white Communion dress. I felt like a bride in my precious gown. Every hair on my head was in place beneath a decorative wreath. I was ready.

My First Communion

The great day finally arrived. The church was filled with white lilies. The pews were packed with family members and friends. In the crowd I saw my grandparents Boeckem and Berti. Even though my father's family was Lutheran, they also came to see my First Communion. Grandma and Grandpa

Bredt and Tante Martha, as well as my cousins Edith and Renate, were all present. Anyone who was not tied up in the war effort or too far away to travel was there that day. As I received my very first communion my heart felt overwhelmed. I could feel Jesus close to me, a very humbling and honoring experience.

After the service, the whole family came over to our small apartment. Mutti had baked seven different cakes, most of them the day before. We sat down and feasted on cake and imitation coffee (real coffee was not available) and laughed and talked for hours. It was a wonderful time, but everything good comes to an end and by evening people began to say their good-byes and travel home again. However, I treasured this day in my memory and replayed it when I needed to think about happier times. Days like this

My neighbor Frau Dudek was one of many who came to my First Communion.

always made other days more bearable as the war progressed.

The following few weeks were relatively routine. The danger of war was always present, but after a while even danger becomes routine. During one stretch of several days beginning on August 31, 1943, we had one air raid after another without pause. I remember they began as usual. I was asleep in bed when the first sirens went off around 2:00 a.m. Mutti jumped up at the sound of the sirens, but was not yet fully awake. She turned to wake me, but she could not remember my name. She said, "Wake up! Wake up! What's your name?" I stared at my mother in disbelief, not knowing whether to laugh or cry. I answered "Erika Bredt." Later it was funny to think about, but at the time it was not funny at all.

During this air raid, our entire city of Rheydt and neighboring city of Moenchengladbach were under attack. Both the industrial areas and the train station across the street were targets. Everyone who lived in our apartment building quickly moved to the cellar, the only place we thought to be safe. The cellar walls where constructed in such a way that in the event of fire or other types of emergency, the walls could be broken through to the adjacent buildings. This was designed to provide a way of escape for people trapped in the cellar.

Once everyone had made their way downstairs, we huddled together, awaiting the all clear signal. Usually, the sounds of the bombs were heard in the distance, and the all clear sounded within an hour. On this night, it felt like the bombs were falling right outside our building all around us. Every time a bomb hit the ground, we felt the earth shake beneath us and saw the building tremble above us. Some people were praying, others were cursing the enemy. The noise outside—the terrible rumbling and the shooting from the airplanes—was deafening, terrifying those who waited for the end to come.

A few of the men in our building were either older or not well enough to fight in the war. They stood by the front door watching what was going on outside and reporting to us inside. They described how the sky was lit up with search lights, the location of fires in the area, and whatever destruction was visible from their vantage point. After what seemed like hours, the all clear siren sounded.

Those in our building survived, our damage limited to several broken windows and cracked or broken interior walls, but others were not so lucky. Around the corner from our building, many homes had been completely destroyed, their residents killed. The middle section of the city was virtually gone. No one had any electricity, and water was scarce. For days and weeks after this particular raid, a dark cloud of smoke covered the sky. People walked around with gas masks covering their faces as the city continued to smolder and burn in places.

After the raid, people walked to the Rheydter Stadium to receive food. The Rheydter Stadium had once been the location for national football games, but those days were long past. The Red Cross used the stadium now to set up large war kitchens to feed those whose homes were destroyed or who could not otherwise get food to feed themselves or their families. It was within walking distance of our home and provided us with a very welcome hot meal on many occasions. Usually, the meal consisted of a hearty soup of meat and potatoes. My favorite meal was Erbensuppe, a thick pea soup rich in flavor, containing large chunks of ham. The Rheydter Stadium also became a place to meet new friends, play, and share both good and bad news with others.

The day following the raid, my grandparents Bredt were concerned about the welfare of family members

As an industrial city in the Ruhr Valley, Rheydt was a strategic target for air raids. The Allied bombing of the city during the war left most of Rheydt destroyed. Rubble filled the streets for weeks and months on end.

living in Moenchengladbach, particularly Opa's nephew Gerhard who was paralyzed from the waist down. Gerhard had suffered from lead poisoning, like Opa, and was now confined to a wheelchair. Communication lines were down and no transportation aside from walking was available. At around noon we began walking in search of information. We were not allowed to start any earlier because Russian prisoners of war were still at work defusing or exploding the bombs which had not detonated on impact the night before. After a long while, we arrived at a large warehouse. It was no longer used to store goods; now it was the place bodies were taken for identification.

As I walked into this room of death, I was horrified. The smell was overwhelming. But the sights were nightmarish. We walked together among the many dead men, women and children, all lying side by side in neat rows. The horrible pictures of what I saw have been forever etched into my memory. To my right, an elderly woman had been decapitated, her head lying face down on her nightgown-clad body. A little farther, I saw a girl about my age. Half her face was missing. She also was wearing her nightgown, with one sock on and the other sock half-off. Body after body lay dismembered, missing an arm or a leg or both. I think we looked at about thirty or forty bodies, before my grandmother took me quickly out again. Fortunately none of our relatives were among the dead. On the return trip, we stopped by the homes of more of our relatives on the Bredt side of the family. Everyone seemed to be accounted for and uninjured, including Gerhard, to the relief of my Opa.

The air raids continued for many days and weeks. We no longer felt safe in our cellar and for quite some time we spent the evenings in a local bomb shelter. The shelter was designed to withstand even the most severe air raid. Hundreds of people, mostly women, children, and the elderly, came to the shelter. The air was sticky and stale, filled with smoke from black market cigarettes. The sound of children crying and people snoring filled the long nights. We slept very little. Mutti could not handle staying in the bomb shelter for long. Soon we returned home and prayed that we would survive each attack. Strangely enough, I was seldom scared during an air raid. It had become a way of life. I had my mother and that was all I needed to feel safe.

12 ~ *Survival*

Throughout the summer and fall of 1943, death and destruction were everyday occurrences. People wondered if the war would ever end. Sometimes in the evening, Mutti and my grandparents Bredt would lean in closely to the small radio and listen to the BBC, an English radio station, for word from the outside. The volume was turned as low as possible because it was forbidden by the Fuehrer to listen to that station; if they were caught, the punishment would be severe.

On a daily basis families buried the bodies of those soldiers killed in battle, or of loved ones caught by a sudden air raid. Some families never received the bodies of their slain—either they died too far away for transport or they remained unknown, too damaged to be identified. Some soldiers did return home, but broken both physically and spiritually. Just as our beautiful city Rheydt lay mostly in ruins, so these men bore the destruction of the war in their own bodies.

I remember one family friend who lived around the corner with his wife and blind son. He returned home from the war after a long stay in the hospital, during which time the surgeons had to amputate one of his legs. It was shocking to see this once healthy young man now an invalid. And he was not the only one. One after another, the walking wounded returned home. But for everyone who came out of the war alive, we knew of many who would never return home. My thoughts frequently turned to Papa, wondering if life would be different if he had simply been wounded, and given the chance to return home.

During this time, Mutti made friends with a very nice couple from the Ukraine, Luba and Imo Schenko. They had been captured by the Nazis and placed in separate work camps near where we lived. We were not allowed to speak or contact them, but many of the local people did so anyway out of compassion for their situation. We had to be very careful not to be caught because the consequences would be severe. Mutti and others shared food with Luba and Imo. Sometimes Mutti snuck Luba out to go to the movies; she would give her clothes to help her look more like a German person. After a while, we lost contact with the Schenkos. They disappeared and we never found out what happened to them.

It was not uncommon to see prisoners of war at work in the streets of Rheydt during the war. Above, prisoners shovel snow off the street in front of the train station.

With the close of 1943 just around the corner, life in Rheydt was more difficult than ever. The war had really taken its toll. Food and most daily necessities were severely rationed; the black market flourished. If someone needed something that was not available in stores, the only option was to trade on the black market. Black market trading involved having something worth trading and knowing the right connections. Money was virtually useless.

That winter was very cold, and coal, our only source for heat, was hard to find. But when people need something, they will usually find a way to get it. Across from our apartment, the train that transported coal to other areas sometimes had to stop at our station for up to an hour. Whenever this would happen, people from our street and nearby streets would come running with buckets in their hands to help themselves to the coal. They'd scramble up the coal car and fill up their buckets. Having coal meant we would be able to cook, take warm baths, and keep our apartment warm.

Sometimes, people were still on top of the coal car when the train unexpectedly began to move. When this happened, the people stuck on the train had to wait until it stopped again a few miles down the track and walk home with their heavy buckets. Having coal was worth the risk—people were willing to take chances in order to survive.

Like everyone else, Mutti and I lived off ration cards. Some foods were scarce; other items nonexistent. Items that had once been important had not been seen in our grocery stores in years. I remember hearing once about bananas. I asked Mutti what a banana tasted like. She thought for a few minutes and then said it was similar to a ripe pear. I hoped one day I would get to taste one.

In December, I turned nine years old. I was now old enough to walk to the market after school and buy our daily groceries. Mutti gave me a small grocery list which I handed to the sales clerk for food items we needed for that day. The shopping bag was made of black braided leather strips and had two handles. If the bag was heavy, it made my fingers stiff and sore. This especially bothered me during the cold weather.

It was not unusual during these hard times for a shortage of vegetables to occur. If someone did not have connections with farmers, or relatives with vegetable gardens, they would pick the wild-growing dandelion to cook like spinach. My mother did this occasionally. I thought it tasted pretty good.

Across the street from our neighborhood store was the bakery. I loved going to the bakery—the aroma of baking breads and cakes made my mouth water. During the last two years of the war, the customary bread made from wheat flour became less and less available. Frequently, the only bread available was made from yellow corn flour. Corn flour bread did not taste as good as our crisp wheat flour bread, but it still smelled wonderful. As I waited for my bread purchase, I gazed hungrily at the few rare cakes and pastries displayed on the shelves. Sugar and chocolate were heavily rationed items. Purchasing certain cakes and pastries at the bakery meant using up much of your monthly allotment of sugar. Few people indulged in this kind of luxury. But it was nice to look!

Now and then Mutti sent me to the train station to buy a bottle of lemonade or sprudel wasser from Otto, a good friend of my father's who worked at the station as a waiter. I looked forward to those times and considered the drink a special treat, because it did not happen often. Otto was a nice young man, but he couldn't walk straight because he was born with a hunchback. His handicap kept him from being drafted into the war. Whenever he saw me he thought of his deceased friend and said, "Erika, you look more and more like Pitter," meaning Peter my father.

As Christmas approached, Mutti had to decide how to spend her "sweet" ration. She could either buy sugar in order to bake a cake for the holidays, or she could buy chocolate as a special treat. She could not buy both. If she bought chocolate, most of the treat would go to Mutti. Because we so seldom had chocolate, I had never developed a taste for it but, for some reason I never understood, Mutti would hide the chocolate anyway in order to keep it for herself.

Even with treats and luxuries so scarce, I was taught from an early age to share and to always take the smaller piece if offered anything to eat. Manners were very important to Mutti. Sometimes I wished my friends had those kinds of manners. Hans-Joseph was the son of one of our neighbors directly adjacent to us. A year older than me, we frequently played together. His family was Swiss and had not received their German citizenship. Frequently, his family received care packages from relatives back in Switzerland. Hans-Joseph would tell me all about the wonderful sweets and pastries he received, and how they tasted in his mouth, and how delicious every last morsel was. His words made my mouth water as I envisioned a vast array of every treat imaginable. I longed for just the tiniest piece of candy or a sliver of my favorite marzipan, but he never of-

My neighbor and friend
Hans-Joseph

fered anything to me. At least he didn't eat it in front of me, but he sure talked about it a lot.

Another friend of mine, Erika Liebermann, lived in the neighboring apartment house. Erika was a few years younger than me and lived with her beautiful mom. Her parents were not married to each other. In fact, her father, an older man, was married to another woman and lived with her in the town of Odenkirchen, the hometown of my grandparents Boeckem, about twenty minutes away by train. Erika's father and his wife owned a bakery in Odenkirchen. Every day he rode the train to Rheydt to visit Erika and her mother, Fraulein Liebermann. Each time he brought with him fresh baked bread, pastries, and broetchen. If I was at her house playing when he arrived, Erika would invite me to have lunch with them. I loved eating "real" bread—it was so good. No wonder I liked playing with Erika so much.

Because the war had been an ongoing event for most of my life, I was probably less affected by the devastation than those who had known what it was like to live in peaceful times. Occasionally, Mutti took me to see the movies. I remember my favorite movie was "Der Graf von Monte Cristo" or "The Count of Monte Cristo." That was a very special day for me. Often during the day, Mutti would sing. She had a beautiful voice, and I loved to sit there and listen to her. Everyone loved to listen as the sound of her voice traveled through the house. Most of her songs were sad and made me cry. But for these few moments, I considered myself a happy child as long as I had my mother close by. She was all I had and I loved her very much.

13 ~ *Adventures with Berti*

Another Christmas approached, and my great wish was to get a doll carriage for my two dolls. I had been fervently wishing and praying for a doll carriage for months. I visualized myself going for long walks after school pushing my dolls in my beautiful doll carriage. I wanted it so bad it was all I could think about. I tried to tell myself it wasn't going to happen; many people have to go without while the war continued, and I was going to be one of them. Then Christmas arrived. Never was there such a happy girl. I don't know how Mutti did it, but there stood the most incredible doll carriage just for me. Immediately, I put my two dolls inside and went for a long walk. I was thrilled.

Taking my dolls for longs walks became a beloved practice. My favorite place to go was a bombed out chapel near the entrance of a cemetery about ten minutes from our street. I carefully climbed through the ruins and cleaned up a small area to play in, creating a little home for my dolls and me. Then I rummaged through the debris looking for broken pieces of the stained glass windows that used to adorn the church. I arranged the glass as decorations in my "home." I spent many happy hours in my pretend home, where everything was peaceful and right.

On other days, I tucked my dolls in their carriage and walked a few blocks to the homes of my school friends, Hildegard Schiffer and Marlene Roebel. The three of us loved to play dolls together. We sewed our own doll dresses by hand and exchanged them with each other. We had some very good times in a very bad time. On my own street, the only children my age were boys, Arthur, Hans-Joseph, and Karl-Heinz. I played with them occasionally, but they didn't want to play with dolls.

My friend Karl-Heinz, when he was a teenager. We lost touch after I moved away from Rheydt

Sometimes my "uncle" Berti, Mutti's younger brother, came to visit us on his bicycle. Because all rubber was used in the war effort, Berti's bicycle did not have any tires. He rode on the bare metal wheels. Whenever he arrived, he would pick me up and I'd ride on the back of his bicycle. Then we'd ride around.

One day, Berti picked me up and planned on riding both of us back to Odenkirchen. However, earlier in the week, the main street to Odenkirchen had been bombed. A huge crater now stood where the road had been. The only way to get around the crater was by crossing a slender sandy patch about 18 inches wide. Berti wanted to ride across the patch; I wanted to find another way. But twelve-year-old Berti decided it would not be a problem for the two of us to ride his bike across the slender patch. I held on tight to Berti as he pedaled within inches of the huge bomb crater. We had almost made it past, when the front wheel slipped on the sandy ground towards the crater. There was nothing we could do but fall into the deep pit, the bike falling on top of us.

Luckily, neither of us was seriously injured. We suffered some scratches and bruises, but were otherwise intact. Berti's bike was twisted and bent. The real problem, however, was figuring out how we were going to get out. The crater was about fourteen feet deep. I was crying but Berti simply thought the entire affair was funny. As we lay there, we heard a sound above us. Someone was approaching the crater. We were so happy, thinking we were about to be rescued, when flying over the edge of the crater came a man and his bicycle, crashing on top of us. Apparently, like Berti, he thought he could ride past the crater as well. Now, all three of us were hurt pretty badly. I don't remember how we got out of that crater, but eventually we made it. Berti and I pushed the totally ruined bike home several miles away. We talked about that day for many years to come.

Early in 1944, Berti and I had another occasion to spend quite a bit of time together. Mutti became very ill and was diagnosed with diphtheria, a very contagious disease. She was going to have to stay in a hospital until she recovered. The question of who was going to care for me came up. My grandparents Bredt both worked during the day. The decision was made to send me to my grandparents Boeckem in Odenkirchen. Mutti was taken to a clinic called "Villa Leise" outside of Rheydt that specialized in the treatment of diphtheria. "Villa Leise" was in a very isolated location to help prevent the spread of the disease. Though I was not allowed to visit Mutti, my grandma would occasionally take me to a spot on the grounds where Mutti and I could see each other. Mutti would wave from her window, and I waved back.

Meanwhile, I had Berti to play with. We spent hours building sand castles in a nearby abandoned castle. Sometimes, Berti allowed me to use his roller skates. In general, Berti and I got along fairly well. Sometimes he could be pretty cruel and sadistic though. He used my grandfather's hunting rifle to shoot worms at close range in the backyard. He enjoyed watching them die, thinking it funny when their wounds turned purple and swelled up. When he was like this, I usually left him and went back inside.

One time he asked me to watch him light up a cigarette. He struck the match and puffed on the butt end of the cigarette until the tip glowed orange. Then he turned to me with a strange smile on his face and said, "Erika, did you know I can blow smoke out of my eyes?" I shook my head, wondering how he was going to make this magic happen. "First you have to close your eyes and put your hand on my chest, and then you will see." Perhaps I was being naive, but I did what he said. I closed my eyes and put my hand on his chest, waiting for him to say "Open your eyes and see the smoke." Instead, while my eyes were closed, Berti pressed the lit cigarette into the top of my hand. I screamed while he laughed. He thought it was very funny.

On another day, Berti and I were playing outside. A beautiful carriage pulled by two black horses came down the street. Inside the carriage, a young couple waved at us as we waved at them. We watched them until they disappeared around the corner. Berti and I were talking about how nice it would be to ride in a carriage like that when suddenly the air raid sirens sounded. We were too far from home to return, so we rushed to a neighbor's house for shelter. Soon, the bombs began to fall. The sound of the exploding bombs grew closer and closer, shaking the ground around us. After a while, the bombing stopped and we were allowed outside again.

Berti and I walked around the next few blocks, examining the damage done to homes, businesses and streets. The area we saw was very badly hit. Whole blocks of houses had been obliterated, the remaining wreckage burning away any semblance of what had existed only moments before. Then suddenly, both of us were shocked by an unexpected sight. The beautiful horse-drawn carriage we had seen shortly before the air raid lay crushed on the ground, the black horses covered with blood and apparently dead. The young couple that had waved at us lay lifeless in the twisted wreckage. One moment, they were happy and carefree, enjoying the beautiful spring day, unaware that their lives were ticking off their final minutes together. How fragile we are, how tenuous each breath, for at any moment, our lives may be swept away without a trace.

Mutti recovered from her diphtheria and came home again after several weeks' stay at the clinic. We resettled in our apartment in Rheydt. During her stay at the clinic, Mutti became close friends with a piano teacher who lived nearby. Later, she came to visit us often in our home. I asked her many questions about playing the piano and she offered to give me free lessons. I don't know why I turned her down, but I did—something I still regret to this day. We lost track of her around the end of the war. Like many others, people moved away or simply seemed to disappear.

During my stay in Grandma Boeckem's house, I had discovered Mutti's old doll. She had long brown pigtails with bangs. Her hair was made from real human hair. Her body was made of porcelain and leather. She was tall with bendable legs and arms. Her name was Mathilde, and she was the only doll Mutti had ever owned. Mutti let me play with her. She also told me to be very careful because the doll was breakable. I played with her a lot and took good care of her. Though I had fun with my grandparents and Berti, I was so happy to be back with my mother. I missed her so much.

After returning home, I contacted my next door friend Hans-Joseph by knocking on the wall that separated our two homes. Minutes later he looked through the window. I told him that we were back home again and arranged to meet downstairs after dinner to catch up on everything that had happened while I was gone. After dinner, I took the fast way down the stairs by sliding down the banister. This always scared Mutti but it was a lot of fun and fast.

I met Hans-Joseph in front of my building and we sat on the concrete steps to talk. In no time, our friend Arthur showed up as well. The three of us decided to look for shrapnel from exploded bombs. Most fragments were about one to two inches long and twisted, with sharp, jagged edges. They were usually bright and shiny. We already had quite a collection. Then we started trading a few small pieces for bigger hard-to-find ones. Every child had a collection. That was the thing to do. Evening came quickly and it was time to return home again. For a very little while, life seemed almost normal.

Hans-Joseph and I riding in a horse-drawn wagon

14 ~ Evacuation to Sadelkow

In the spring of 1944, we received notification from the German authorities to evacuate to a safer part of Germany farther from most of the war activity. It was simply too dangerous to remain in the Ruhr Valley. Within days all young mothers and their children had to pack their belongings and meet at the main train station in Rheydt. From there, we would be transported to a small town called Sadelkow near Mecklenburg in northern Germany. I was very sad to leave my home and my grandparents Bredt, but we had no choice.

The journey to Sadelkow took all day. Once we arrived, we were met by military people who helped us get settled. Mutti and I were assigned to live with a family named Sternhagen. The Sternhagens lived on a farm with their extended family: grandparents,

parents, and children all lived together. They also had a German shepherd dog. Thankfully, the house was large, so Mutti and I had a room to ourselves. Aside from this one thing we shared, in every other way, we became a part of the family, with our own daily chores.

The Sternhagens had a ten-year-old daughter named Lilli. She also had major responsibilities in the family. She helped work in the fields and milked the cows. Occasionally, Lilli and I played together. Once again I had to learn to walk barefoot, which was not the most pleasant experience when playing among the chickens, roosters, and other livestock. I never quite got used to the feeling of excrement squishing up between my toes. Once again I stumbled over rocks and gravel, scraping my toes until they bled. Lilli and I would also play in the barn where the horses and cows were sheltered. We enjoyed climbing into the hay-covered loft and watching the mice run up the walls.

While staying with the Sternhagens, I also attended school. It was there that I learned about the entire process of making silk. The classroom was filled with open cages, each containing silk caterpil-

During our first evacuation, Mutti and I stayed with the Sternhagen family in northern Germany. Ten-year-old Lilli, standing beside me above, became my good friend.

lars (Seidenraupen). We watched the caterpillars wrap themselves up in a substance excreted from their own bodies. Over time, this substance becomes silk. The whole process was very interesting, reminding me of how a spider builds its nest.

After several months of living with the Sternhagens, we received word that Rheydt had returned to relative safety. We were permitted to return home, at least temporarily. We said our good-byes to the Sternhagens, and began the journey home. I was so happy to see my grandparents once again, and to visit the places I knew and loved.

Left: the Sternhagen children with me in the front middle;
Right: Mutti and I standing in front of our temporary home during our first evacuation

Upon returning, I discovered that my former school building had been partially destroyed by a firebomb. The instability of the remaining structure made it unsafe for us to return. Therefore, all the students in the first through eighth grades were reassigned to another school about thirty minutes walk away, right around the corner from my Tante Martha's home. I was able to visit her often. Our longtime teacher Miss Kloeckner went with us to the new school.

Our new school was in the opposite direction from our old school. We passed several interesting stores on the way, my favorite being the butcher shop. Often, my friends and I would stop and purchase blood wurst. It was cheap and tasted delicious to me. Occasionally, our stops ran us late to school. In order to make up the time, we took forbidden short cuts by crossing over many railroad tracks, saving us about ten minutes. If caught doing this, which happened on a couple of occasions, we were in big trouble.

At school, religion was no longer a part of our assignments. We were not given a reason for this change to our studies. Our priest simply no longer came to class as he had done in the past. About this same time, another one of our priests, Pater Hutmacher, a very well-liked and outspoken person, disappeared one night. It was rumored that he had preached against the Nazis from the pulpit. Somehow the word reached the officials. We never found out who reported him, but one day he simply vanished. We never heard from him again.

15 ~ *Living with the Hahns*

We had been home only a few months when once again we were notified to leave our home and move to a safer region in Eastern Germany. The air strikes and bombings by the Allies were very close to our home, with the heaviest fighting occurring near Venlo and Aachen, on the border with Holland. All young mothers with children were ordered to evacuate. Once again, Mutti and I packed our clothes and our few belongings, said good-bye to our friends and family, and walked to the train station. There we joined many other women and children who would journey with us to a place further from danger. Each family was placed wherever there was available space.

Mutti and I boarded a train eastbound for a town called Haldensleben, near the city of Magdeburg. Like all the trains, this one was packed. Many trains had been destroyed during the war, and others were used primarily by the military, so the few available trains were in high demand. Seating was rare; many people simply climbed on top of the coal cars to escape the danger. There was little organization or order. People were afraid and reacted out of their fear.

Once the train began moving, it took us a couple of days to reach our destination. Sometimes the train stopped for hours because the tracks were damaged by bombings. The train also stopped if an air raid began. Eventually, the sounds and sights of war diminished as we moved farther east. Finally, we reached Haldensleben. There, families had been ordered to give up one extra room in their home and take in the evacuees. Most of these families were farmers.

Mutti and I were assigned to live with two related families who jointly owned and operated one large farm. Strangely enough, both families' last names rhymed. Herr and Frau Hahn had two grown daughters living with them. The first was single and in her twenties—I called her Fraulein Hahn. The other was married to a man with the last name of Zahn. They had two daughters: Eleven-year-old Ingrid and nine-year-old Thea. The farm was also home to many animals, including a pretty

I enjoyed playing with the Zahn family cat

Erika, Ingrid, Mutti, Thea and her mother Frau Zahn

Calico cat. Mutti and I were shown to a clean and nicely furnished room with one bed for the both of us. I never minded sharing a bed with Mutti. That first night we were exhausted, and slept soundly till morning.

After dressing the following morning, we joined the family for a breakfast of boiled eggs. This became our morning routine. However, during lunch time we met with other evacuees and ate in a restaurant. There, we shared what little information we had from home. Mutti and I also discovered a small Catholic church. We began attending Sunday Mass with many of the other friends we met. During the week, I began attending school in order to keep up with my studies. The rest of our time was spent taking long walks in the country, or exploring the forests. There was not much to do and all we had was time.

Over the next few months, I became good friends with Thea. About a year younger than myself, I remember her as a very nice girl who was easy to get along with. We would spend our time playing with

Thea and I playing with our dolls

our dolls and sewing doll clothes by hand. I felt happy and safe while living at Thea's home. After a time, we began to hear rumors that the war would be coming to an end very soon. While we waited for the news that would allow us to return to Rheydt, we quietly celebrated Mutti's thirtieth birthday on March 11,

1945. It seemed like the future was going to be brighter for us both.

One day, something very funny happened at the Hahn's home. Mutti and I had returned home from church one Sunday in time to have dinner with Herr and Frau Hahn. The meal was like a feast—we had not seen that much food in a long time. Dinner began with a rich vegetable soup. When Frau Hahn brought the soup, the wonderful aroma filled the room as the steam rose tantalizingly from the bowl. My mouth watered at the delicious scent. Mutti and I began to sip the hot delicious soup, as the rest of the guests laughed and talked, when something caught our eye. I don't remember who noticed it first, but we both became aware that something strange was in Mr. Hahn's soup. We tried to look without drawing attention to ourselves. Sure enough, Mr. Hahn's vegetable soup had a worm in it.

Mutti looked at me and I looked at her and we didn't know what to do or say. If we brought attention to the worm, we would have insulted the lady of the house and her wonderful cooking. Everyone's appetite would have been ruined. Yet, if we said nothing, what would happen to Mr. Hahn and his worm? We sat there quiet as two mice as we secretly watched him finish every last drop of soup, completely unaware of the uninvited guest. Years later, Mutti and I would talk about that event and laugh.

Our time in Haldensburg was short, but memorable. One day we heard a rumor that a train carrying supplies for the German army had stopped at the train station and would not be continuing its journey. The American military was approaching; therefore car after car of food was available to the evacuated families in order to keep it out of the hands of the enemy.

Mutti and I hurried to the station in time to see hundreds of women and children crawling like ants all over the food cars. People were falling on top of each other; children were crying. It was a scary sight for a ten-year-old. Mutti charged right into the middle of the chaos in order to take some of the food. She filled her arms with whatever she could hold, fought her way back to me to safeguard her store, and then dove back into the melee for more. Mutti gathered lots of food, mainly canned goods like marmalade, meat, and powdered eggs, as well as butter, bread and more.

Watching the people from the sidelines became quite entertaining. At one point, two women began fighting over a large barrel of marmalade. Each claimed it as hers, but neither was willing to give up the barrel to the other. Finally, one of the women became so angry, that she took the open barrel of sticky marmalade and poured it over the other woman's head. It was an unforgettable moment, and I sat there shocked and thoroughly amused by the lengths to which people would go in desperate situations.

After a while, Mutti had gathered all the food she could. I don't know how we were able to carry all the cans and boxes back to the Hahn farm, but somehow we managed. For many days after that, Mutti cooked scrambled eggs and meat on a little hotplate in our room. She served it with bread and lots of marmalade. It always made me smile to remember the woman with marmalade dripping down her face.

16 ~ *Escape to the West*

Days later the Americans moved in and the war was over. American soldiers armed with various weapons could be seen on every street corner. One particular G.I. sat on his helmet on the street corner across from our window every day. It must have been his assigned corner. At some point, he must have noticed my mother because he stared at the window quite often. As far as I know, they never actually came in contact with one another. We were not allowed to go outside. At first I was afraid, but after a few days, I became used to the presence of these foreigners. As long as we obeyed the rules, we had nothing to fear.

Since the war was now over, Mutti and I wanted to return home to Rheydt. However, unlike during the war, now we were on our own. No one was in charge of making sure we had transportation back to our home. The Hahn family was very kind and supportive during this time. They made sure we knew we were welcome to stay as long as we needed; they did not push us to move. Then something happened that made leaving a priority. The Russians arrived, closing all the main borders back into the west.

Unlike the American soldiers, the Russians were loud and obnoxious. They frequently drank late into the night, and didn't think twice about harassing the local citizens. They established a strict curfew; we were only allowed to go outside during the day time and only for certain hours.

With the borders closed, Mutti and I didn't know how to return home. Mutti discussed the situation with our landlord. He knew of a road outside of town that was still open to travel. We quickly packed our belongings and followed Mr. Hahn outside of town to a path that led back to the west side. We couldn't cross until dark, so we hid on the front porch of another family's home, waiting for night to fall. By early evening, it was dark enough to travel and we started on our escape when we heard the sound of a horse and cart coming toward us. Fearful of the Russians, I breathed a sigh of relief to see it was just a farmer carrying other evacuees. He pulled up alongside us and said that this border crossing was also closed. They had been turned away by the Russian soldiers.

Disappointed, we carried our belongings back to the porch and wondered what we should do. We were homeless and scared, with no idea of how we could get back to Rheydt, to our family and friends. We tried to sleep that night on the porch. To our dismay, directly across the street from our hiding place was a large warehouse that had become a temporary quarters for the Russian soldiers. All night long they drank and made a terrible ruckus. Mutti and I held on to each other, quietly crying and afraid of what might happen if we were discovered. We knew we would be in immediate trouble for not obeying the curfew. Also, Mutti was a beautiful young woman. The Russian soldiers wouldn't hesitate to take advantage of a helpless German woman.

Finally, just before the dawn, Mutti and I experienced a miracle. We had not slept all night, and we were cold and stiff from hiding on the porch. The Russians had apparently finally fallen asleep because the warehouse was now quiet. At about six o'clock, we heard someone walking by fairly close to where we were huddled together. We held our breath as the footsteps grew closer. We did not know who might be coming this way. Then, a whispered voice called out to us. We looked up and to our surprise we saw the kindly face of a nun. She had been walking to church when she discovered us huddled on the porch.

She told us to follow her to the home of another family she knew. There, we were able to get cleaned up and get something to eat. It was so nice to be away from that warehouse and those Russian soldiers. After eating, the family told us of a secret passage across the border. A plan was made to wait until dark and then try to make our escape through this new passage.

That evening, once again, we gathered our belongings together. Mutti and I hid in a horse drawn wagon, as the farmer drove through the woods to an isolated area not yet discovered by the Russians. There in the woods was a hidden passageway back into the west zone. We thanked the farmer, gathered our belongings, and quickly crossed over with a few others. We had barely made it across to the west side, when we heard shouting behind us. Looking back, we saw Russian soldiers running to stop those who were following after us. The Russians had discovered the passageway. Several people, traveling only minutes behind Mutti and myself, were captured and forced to return to the east side. This last opening into the west was then blocked by the soldiers, but thankfully, we were safe from the Russians.

Once on the west side, everything became a blur. I don't remember how we arrived at the train station or how long it took to travel back to Rheydt. All I remember is how it seemed like a horrible neverending dream. I do remember my shock upon arriving at Rheydt. The city had been totally destroyed by the war. What were once massive brick buildings and stores and apartments now lay in piles of rubble and glass and dirt on the broken streets. My street was one of very few that missed a direct hit by a bomb.

Allied forces arrive in Rheydt in the spring of 1945

Even so, walls were cracked and windows broken. Glass was everywhere. Thankfully, my Grandma and Grandpa Bredt were both alive and doing well. All my relatives were safe and alive. God had spared our family the devastation that had been borne by so many others.

Even though our home came through the war relatively unscathed, things were far from normal. At first, the English soldiers occupied Rheydt; they were polite but distant. However, then the Russians arrived. Once again, we were put on a twenty-four hour curfew and not allowed to leave our homes. Those who disobeyed the curfew were severely punished. Reports of women being raped and homes being desecrated were common. Finally, the day arrived when the Russians left. We rejoiced at their departure; they left many bad memories in the minds of many of the German people.

Other parts of our lives changed as well with the end of the war. We had very little money and very little to buy. For some time we lived on ration cards until the economy got back on its feet. Trading on the black market thrived. After quite a while, some food imports began arriving. I remember during this time I ate my first banana. After several months, our German soldiers who had survived were released from prison camps and came home, some bearing life-changing injuries. One of these soldiers was my Onkel Josef. Both his legs and his right arm were badly wounded. Eventually, his legs returned to normal, but for the rest of his life, his arm remained stiff. It was reset in a hospital into an "L" shape in order to appear normal. Many soldiers did not come home at all.

With the return of the men, the clean-up of the city began. Everyone helped, including the very old and the very young, shoveling debris into buckets, clearing the streets, and restoring homes. People worked without pay, volunteering their time from morning until evening, seven days a week. We were so happy to be alive and that the war was finally over and we were home where we belonged.

About this time, we finally learned what had happened to the Jewish people and others in the concentration camps. We were horrified to read that Dachau, the prison camp we had passed by during one of our trips to Emmering, was the location of so much death and destruction. I remembered walking by the gates of Dachau, and now wondered if at that moment innocent people were being murdered.

Dachau was the first Concentration Camp in Germany. Originally an abandoned munitions factory from World War I, it became the last "home" for thousands of prisoners from all over Europe, and a training ground for murder. Inmates in Dachau included political opponents to the Nazi party, gypsies, clergymen who resisted the political coercion of the churches, and many average German citizens who made critical remarks of various kinds regarding the Nazi regime. All these prisoners were treated with cruelty by the camp guards, but it was the Jewish prisoners who received the worse treatment. During the war, the Jewish prisoners were abused, tortured, and systematically exterminated. A prisoner's day was filled with work, hunger, exhaustion, and fear of the brutality of the sa-

Two ovens inside the crematorium at Dachau

distic guards. Prisoners who fell ill were routinely executed. Often, those who were not exterminated succumbed to starvation.

When the Dachau camp was liberated in April 1945, the help arrived too late for many prisoners. They had died of hunger. News of these atrocities shocked the average German citizen. Some refused to believe it was true until the photographs began circulating. I thought of Luba and Imo Schenko, the nice Ukrainian couple to whom my mother and others gave food. I thought of my neighbor Julius who had taught me to ride a bike. I thought of Pater Hutmacher, the priest who had spoken out against the Nazi Party. I thought of all the people who had simply vanished without a trace and wondered if they had been taken to a place like Dachau. It seemed like the horrors of the war kept on coming, even after it was over.

17 ~ *Moving to Bavaria*

Time went by, and people tried to get their lives back to normal, but everywhere the signs of war were evident. I returned to school on a regular schedule. Fraulein Kloeckner no longer taught our class; she was replaced by Herr Steinert. Twice a week our local pastor taught catechism for the Catholic students; the rest of the students either attended a different class or were dismissed for the day.

People simply made the best of what they had. I remember visiting on several occasions a man who was a friend of both Mutti and my Tante Martha. He lived in an abandoned train

Mutti seated in front of the abandoned train car that served as a "summer house"

My class picture for the school year 1946-47 in Rheydt. I am kneeling in the center with two braids.

coach that had suffered burn damage from the war. The coach, or "summer house" as it was now called, was tucked away in the woods.

One day, while my mother and I were visiting him, I had an experience I will never forget. I was offered my first cup of real coffee. I was excited to get to taste this drink I had heard so much about and sipped the hot steamy liquid. Within minutes, what had been a wonderful momentous occasion became one of the worst experiences of my life. My head began to pound with pain, and I became incredibly sick with a migraine headache. My mother had to take me home where I lay sick for days with the migraine. I thought I was going to die. Finally, the pain subsided, but the experience left an indelible mark in my memory.

Slowly, Mutti began to socialize with other people her age. She seemed to be happy again. She even started to date occasionally, but nothing serious came of these dates and the relationships did not last very long. I remember one man who came regularly to our house to visit Mutti. Fred Fecke owned a driving school in Rheydt. He seemed very smitten with Mutti. Though he was nice to me, I did not care much for him. The fact that Grandma Bredt liked him as well made it difficult for me. It was hard on me to share anybody with Mutti. Most of my young life it was only the two of us and we went through so much. When the relationship ended after a few months, I was more than happy.

Mutti had stayed in touch with her friend Frau Zillner in Emmering, Bavaria, and during the summer of 1947 planned a short vacation to see her again. This time she chose not to take me with her. Instead, she made arrangements to send me to a summer camp for the week. It would be the first time in my eleven years that I would be away from Mutti. Even when she was sick and I stayed with my grandparents Boeckem, I at least was allowed to see her from her hospital window. I was excited to go to summer camp, but I also felt uneasy to be without her.

I am on the left acting silly as my friends and I prepare to leave for summer camp

The day I was supposed to leave for summer camp, I put on my backpack and walked to school to meet the other girls who were also going. Our Catholic pastor had arranged for us to travel by both train and bus to reach our destination. Though initially apprehensive over leaving Mutti, I ended up having a great time at summer camp. We played lots of outside games, walked a lot and had fun. I arrived back home to stay with my grandparents Bredt until Mutti returned from her trip.

While I was at camp, Mutti left on her day long train trip to Munich, Bavaria. Once arriving in Munich, she changed trains to Fuerstenfeldbruck. From there, she had to walk another mile to get to Emmering. While she was gone, Mutti wrote often and sent me a beautiful postcard featuring a girl around my age before a striking mountain background. After a couple of weeks Mutti returned back home with some unexpected news. She had met a man named Karl Koegl who was a good friend of Frau Zillner. Karl had suffered from a head injury during the war and been discharged in the spring of 1945 from the German army. He was seven years older than Mutti and had never been married.

Karl fell in love with Mutti almost immediately upon meeting her. Mutti told us that he wanted her to move to Bavaria. Mutti didn't know what to do. She liked Karl but was not in love with him. However, she also was tired of being alone and poor. Karl offered both companionship and security. Karl's parents had recently passed away, leaving him their house, but hardly any furniture. Mutti had no house, but plenty of furniture. Practically thinking, the arrangement made sense.

Mutti didn't know what to do and spent hours thinking through her decision. She told me she thought in time she could grow to love Karl. He was a good man and would do anything for her. After talking to her own parents, my father's parents, and Tante Martha, she decided to move our little family to Bavaria.

That summer, we packed all our belongings in preparation for the trip south. All of Mutti's belongings and all the furniture was loaded into the moving truck and brought to the train station for the move. It was hard to say good-bye to all our relatives and friends, especially Oma and Opa and Tante Martha. Mutti and I had our own freight car and we traveled together with all of our belongings. That freight car became our "temporary home" over the next several days until we would arrive in Munich.

The train stopped frequently on layovers and to pick up or drop off passengers. During each stop, one of the train conductors checked in with us to see if everything was okay. It did not take me long to see that he was interested in my young, beautiful, widowed mother. Mutti noticed that the conductor was quite handsome as well. Soon, he came to check on us more and more often. On every stop he spent time talking to Mutti. He asked my mother why she was moving so far away from her home, and if he could see her again after she was settled. Mutti told him about Karl, the man she was going to marry but did not love. During our final night on the train, I was awakened by the sound of giggling and whispering. I recognized the voices of the conductor and my mother. He stayed with her in our freight car most of the night.

The next day, as we approached our destination, Mutti told me she was in love with the conductor and the wedding with Karl was off. The conductor was assigned to another freight car going back home as soon as we arrived at our final destination. Mutti and the conductor exchanged addresses, promising to write to one another and continue their relationship. Now Mutti faced the unpleasant prospect of telling Karl that she had met another man on the way to Emmering to marry him. After unloading all our belongings from the train, and transporting them to Karl's home, I finally met the man who was supposed to be my future stepfather.

Karl was overjoyed to see Mutti again. He acted like a nervous young schoolboy around her; he could not believe she was finally there to marry him. I noticed immediately that although Karl was not very good-looking, he seemed like a decent enough man. Hearing that I was hungry after the long journey, he hurried to make me a sandwich, ready to do anything to please us. Both Mutti and I knew that the moment must come when Mutti had to tell him that the wedding was off. Later that evening, she broke the news to Karl. I remember watching him cry like a baby at the news, shaking his head in disbelief. That night, Mutti and I slept at Frau Zillner's house.

Mutti told Frau Zillner all about the wonderful man she had met on the train. We eagerly waited the day his letter would arrive. Each day, Mutti watched for the mail man, but no letter came. Days and then weeks went by, and Mutti became more and more dis-

Karl and Nelly Koegl, taken around 1954.

couraged when nothing arrived by mail from the man she believed she loved. As the summer drew to a close, Mutti had to face the truth. She came to the conclusion that she had been used, that the conductor had no intention of contacting her again. Her heart was broken by what she considered his betrayal. Karl was there to help her through this painful experience. He still loved my mother, and was more than willing to give their relationship another try.

Mutti married Karl Koegl on October 31, 1947. The church wedding was beautiful. Frau Zillner's niece sang in her beautiful soprano voice "So nim denn meine Haende und fuehre mich," which means "take my hands and lead me to the end." As Karl and Mutti exchanged their vows, anyone could see how much Karl adored my mother. His face beamed with happiness. Afterwards, we celebrated at the Zillner's house with many other people.

18 ~ A New Home

Emmering was now my home. It was a beautiful village. The streets were lined with large shady trees, and the river Amper meandered through the village through a thickly wooded area. My new school was less than one mile away and the Catholic Church was about a block from the school. To get to either, we walked, crossing three bridges as we enjoyed the clean fresh smell of the Amper.

Karl's house was a large two-story with a basement and a spacious attic, where I often spent time playing or studying for my school assignments. Both the upstairs and the downstairs each contained three rooms and a non-flushing toilet. In the backyard, the attached washhouse held a large woodburning stove, a chicken coop, and many rabbit cages. Outside, Karl kept a beautiful flower and vegetable garden with blue spruce trees and a variety of bushes.

Karl, whom I now called Papa, leased out part of his home to refugees from East Germany. They had difficulty finding another place to live, so temporarily we were staying in one room with a large closed-off balcony on the upper floor. The large sliding window

My new home in Emmering with my new "Papa"

measured about ten to twelve feet wide, opening from left to right to reveal a large open field. In the distance you could see and hear the Amper River. A large apple tree was braced against the window. During summer and fall I could reach out and pick delicious ripe apples. I slept on the sofa while Mutti and Papa slept in a tiny bed, not much larger than a twin sized bed today. Many refugees from the east side had tried to find a place to live in Emmering. Near the woods, temporary shelters had been set up, but still more places were needed. Every homeowner was required to take in one or more families if they had space available.

The other half of upper floor of Papa's house was rented by a family named Koeniger. They had three children, Gabi age 12, Peter age 13, and Ursula age 18. Ursula became a close friend of mine. The lower floor was rented out by the Blum family of four, including one child and an uncle. After a few months, the Koenigers found a permanent place to stay and moved out. We stayed good friends with them for many years. The entire upper floor now belonged to us exclusively, giving us much more room. We now had a living area with kitchen, two bedrooms, and a bathroom.

Papa's beautiful garden

The Blum family and we shared the water pump located on the bottom floor. We also shared the basement. However, there was no bathtub or shower. Once again we had to carry the water upstairs and use the portable bathtub to get washed and cleaned up. Once a week, usually on Saturdays, we visited an open bathhouse in Fuerstenfeldbruck to take a shower. You purchased your ticket and usually the wait was long. It was kept clean, but smelled musty in the high humidity conditions.

Papa also raised one rooster, about half a dozen chickens to provide us with fresh eggs daily, and many beautiful rabbits. For a short while, we even had a goat for milk. I loved the rabbits and tried to adopt them as my pets, however, my "pets" were raised for food on holidays. Once I watched Papa kill one of the rabbits and it made me sick to my stomach; I never watched again. On another occasion, I watched how he killed a chicken by chopping off its head. I was horrified to see the headless body of the chicken running the yard while the eyes on the separated head continued to move.

To relax, Papa loved to take long walks in the wooded area near our home. He enjoyed nature and usually came home with an armload of mushrooms he had picked. Papa was very knowledgeable about mushrooms, and able to discern which were edible and which were poison. Whenever Papa brought home his mushrooms, Mutti fried them with onions, pepper and salt, and then served them over noodles. It was delicious! During one of Papa's walks into the woods, he did not return home at the usual time. Mutti grew worried. Finally, she took her bicycle and rode into the woods searching for him. She found him lying among the trees and mushrooms, unconscious. Mutti had quite a scare because Papa looked as though he were dead. The ambulance came and took him to the hospital where he spent several days under observation. We never did find out why he lost consciousness.

In June of 1948, the currency we had been using, the reichsmark, was finally replaced with the deutschemark. Each person received forty D-marks. It was stunning to see how practically overnight the stores in town suddenly filled with an abundance of merchandise. Shelves that had long been empty now were filled with all kinds of goods. Many of the items had not been seen in the stores in years. At the same time, the black market seemed to vanish. This change brought with it an overall change in attitude as well. People began to feel more optimistic and hopeful about the future. Most believed the bad times were really behind us and it was time to make plans for the future.

I returned to school almost immediately after settling in Emmering. I knew many of my classmates from our previous trip to the Zillner's home during the war. My new teacher, Herr Bierling, was very strict. However, because I was one of the top students, he liked me. The boys in the class didn't have it so easy. Herr Bierling demanded respect as well as completed homework. If you misbehaved, you were whipped. No misbehavior was tolerated, and the boys seemed to push Herr Bierling to his limit on a daily basis.

My eighth grade classroom in Emmering.
I am in the back row, third from the right near the window.

One part of Herr Bierling's class that the girls enjoyed the most was gazing at his assistant teacher whenever possible. He was a young, very handsome man who was in his first year of teaching. Tall, with wavy brown hair, we girls affectionately called him "Uncle" Franz. We used to tease him until he blushed from embarrassment. We all had a huge crush on him.

My new school was made up of almost all Catholic students. Twice weekly, the Catholic priest, an older, pleasant man came to teach us catechism. The few students who were not Catholic were allowed to go home during the catechism class. Every Wednesday morning at seven o'clock, we also attended mass before going to class. We were not allowed to eat breakfast on those days in order to accept communion. Frequently, the lack of food made me dizzy, and I had to sit down to avoid fainting. Once we arrived at class, we were served a hot lunch. My favorite meal was a crispy hot roll called Semmel and a steaming cup of hot chocolate. I also really enjoyed the rich pea stew served with potatoes and beef. School usually ended at two o'clock. On Saturdays, we were dismissed at one o'clock.

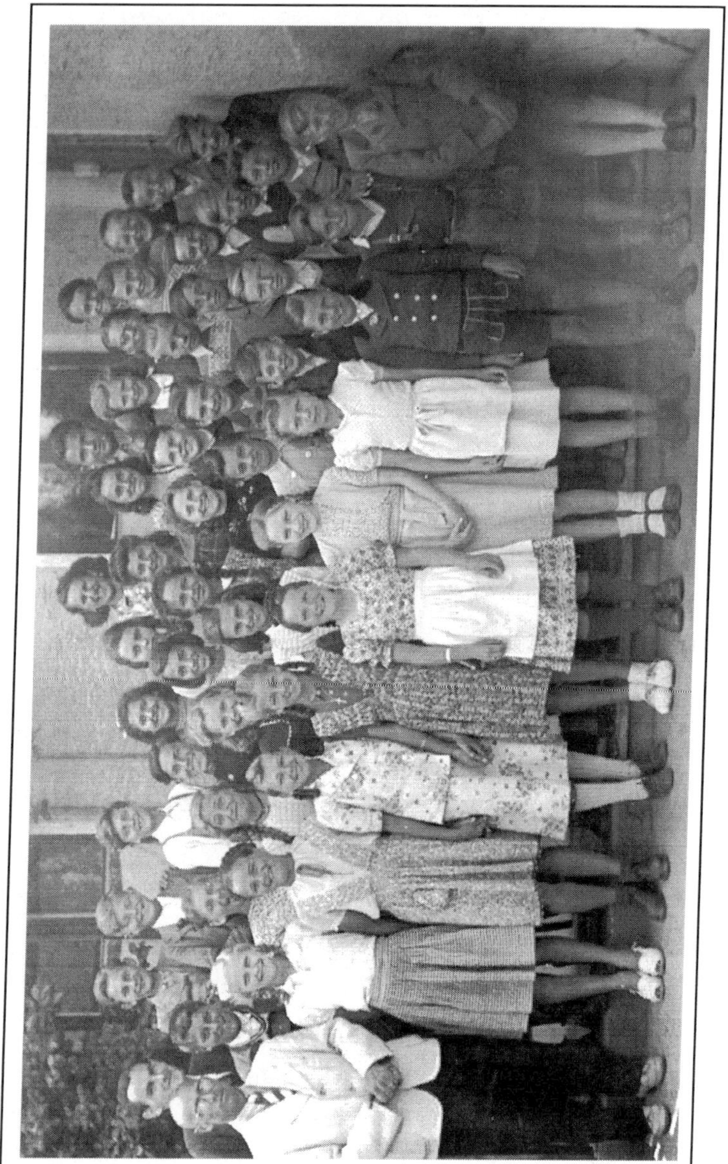

I enjoyed my new school and learned quite a bit. My favorite subject was Math. My father had been a bookkeeper before the war, so I believe I inherited my proficiency with numbers from him. Though a good student, I still had trouble with memorizing and writing essays. My dear friend Ursula Koeniger, whom I called Uschi, helped me with memorizing and writing. She was the daughter of one of the tenants that had shared our house for a while after I first arrived in Emmering. She later became a teacher.

About the time I began going to school in Emmering, the class was getting ready for the Christmas school play. I was selected to participate in the play. A young girl who was destined to become a great friend of mine was also cast in a major role. Margit had moved to Bavaria as part of the wave of refugees that flooded the area in 1946. Margit's family originated from German people who had been living in what is now the Czech Republic. When the Russians occupied the area after the war, they fled to Bavaria. Margit, a very good student, lived with her parents and two sisters in a newly developed area for refugees called the Baracken, situated in a large open area near the Amper River. The homes were plain and simple, distinguishable by their flat roofs.

When Margit was selected along with myself to be in the school play, I was excited. It was the story of a rich family with servants and a poor single mother with a child who had to struggle to make ends meet. I played the rich woman and Margit was chosen to play the poor mother. Though I was happy to have an important role, I was also very fearful because of the horrible time I had with memorization. But I refused to give up. Though it meant suffering through multiple headaches, and a lot of hard work and determination, I learned all my lines. I was never someone who gave up easily. After weeks of rehearsing, the performance was now only days away.

The evening before our last rehearsal I met a very good looking boy named Leo. He had dark wavy hair and soft brown eyes. He was about my age—thirteen years old. His folks had moved to Emmering from Italy and now owned a small farm just on the outskirts of town. I had noticed Leo before actually meeting him. Our eyes would occasionally meet when we passed in the street or at school. He had also noticed me, but had been too shy to approach me until this night.

Leo asked if he could walk me home after rehearsal had finished. I said yes, my heart beating hard. I couldn't believe this handsome guy was interested in me. It was just getting dark as we walked toward my home. As we approached the front door of the house, Leo stopped, put his arms around me, and kissed me gently on the lips. He softly said, "Good night, Erika," and then he was gone. I was shocked and excited at the same time. This was the first time I had ever been kissed by a boy. I looked forward to seeing him again and wondered what would happen next.

Though the performance of the play was a huge success, my relationship with Leo was not. Over the next days and weeks, I saw him occasionally. We'd smile at each other, but that was all. We were too young to date, so our "relationship" didn't go any farther than that first kiss. Frequently I saw him passing my house on his horse and wagon to work on his parents' farm. He was such a hard worker for such a young boy. I felt sad that I didn't get a chance to know him better.

After my experience with Leo, I became more and more interested in boys. Opportunities for boys and girls to spend time together became more frequent. A favorite activity was to get together after school and go sledding. We had a particular hill we'd meet at and have snowball fights, or the boys would sometimes rub snow in the girls' faces. During warm days, we might go swimming in the Amper River. I had never learned to swim and had to be very careful not to go too far out into the current. Fun and happy memories grew more prevalent as the war slowly became part of the past and not the present.

Our play: I am second from the left. Margit is on the far right.

19 ~ A New Family

The marriage between Mutti and my stepfather did not go well at all. Soon after the wedding, the fighting began. Mutti and Papa had huge arguments in which they yelled quite a bit. Papa had a terrible temper, but Mutti was not one to back down. She could raise her voice as loudly as he could. During these times, I tried to either leave the house, or stay out of their way. After a while, the fighting would stop, and we would have a calm period. Sometimes this period of peace would last several weeks before the next onslaught. Though these arguments were often very angry, my stepfather never raised a hand against Mutti. He really did love her.

Papa's temper sometimes seemed abnormal. Over the years, he checked in and out of the hospital due to the head injury he received during the war. I wondered if his head injury might have contributed to his terrible rages. The hardest thing to deal with was how unpredictable his attacks were. He could be incredibly nice one minute, and then the next minute become enraged over the smallest incident.

One Christmas Eve, Mutti and Papa invited the Koeniger family to the house to visit. I had just turned thirteen years old. We were having a great time playing Parcheesi and laughing, when everything suddenly went wrong. Papa was smoking a cigar, which he liked to do on special occasions. During the game, he accidentally dropped his cigar onto the game board, knocking the playing pieces out of their positions. Papa quickly put the pieces back, but I noticed that he had put his piece in a better position than it had previously been. I made the huge mistake of pointing out his error to him.

Papa's face became beet red with anger. I knew what was coming and could do nothing to stop it. He grabbed me by the arm and began beating me in front of everyone. Over and over, he hit me. He wouldn't stop. The others tried to pull him away and finally he relented. Needless to say, the Koenigers quickly left after witnessing that outburst. The following day, I was covered with bruises. It was a Christmas I will never forget. I ached all over. This was not the only time Papa lost control. He often alleviated his frustration over minor incidents by hitting me.

Papa also fought constantly with his tenants. The thing that seemed to irritate him the most was whenever one of the tenants slammed the door as they came in or left the house. On one occasion, Papa, Mutti and I were all in the backyard with one of the tenants. Soon, Papa and the tenant began to argue. The argument escalated until Papa was furious. Suddenly, Papa's face contorted and foam gathered around his mouth.

A little away from the house, we had a brick chicken coop with a ladder leading to the coop. The ladder was secured to the coop by a heavy metal hook attached to the bricks. In his rage, Papa began purposefully running towards the brick coop and the large hook, his head down like a raging bull. We all watched, momentarily frozen as we realized his intentions. No one moved. Then suddenly, at the last possible second, I jumped forward and pushed him aside. I don't know where my strength came from, but he missed the hook and ran into the brick wall at a reduced speed. He was still badly injured, with blood streaming from his head. A little later, he checked into the hospital once again. Though he never mentioned it, I am sure I saved his life that day.

After Papa came home from the hospital, things stayed calm for a while. Every morning at 7:30 he rode his bicycle to the air base at Fuerstenfeldbruck, where he worked as a painter. About this time, Mutti found out she was pregnant. Papa was so happy, he wept for joy. For the duration of her pregnancy, Papa did everything possible for Mutti. He was thrilled to become a father for the first time at the age of forty-one. At the same time, we learned on the radio that Queen Elizabeth was also pregnant. She and Mutti were expecting their babies at the same time. I was so excited that Mutti was pregnant. After losing Manni, I desperately wanted another brother or sister.

Mutti remained active throughout her entire pregnancy despite bouts of morning sickness and unending heartburn. Throughout that summer and fall, Mutti rode her bicycle daily, even during storms. As her due date drew closer, we wondered who would give birth first—Mutti or Queen Elizabeth. Then, a few days before her due date, Mutti went to see her doctor for a routine examination. Dr. Stanik became concerned about the position of the baby. Something was not right. She recommended that Mutti travel to a special clinic in Munich, about seventeen miles from Emmering, for the birth of the baby.

A few days later, Mutti went into labor. Papa nervously crossed the street to use the neighbor's phone to call a taxi. Our neighbor, the mayor of Emmering, was the only person nearby who owned a phone. When the taxi arrived, Papa and Mutti rode off to the special clinic in Munich for the delivery. I stayed home, listening to the radio for the latest news about Queen Elizabeth. Later I learned from Papa that Mutti did not make it to the hospital. While in the taxi, the baby began to be born. The taxi driver frantically tried to make it to the hospital, but the baby had other plans. As Mutti pushed, the baby's feet came out first. The baby was breech and wouldn't come out any farther. Mutti was screaming and Papa was yelling at the driver to hurry. The taxi careened into the hospital parking lot even as the baby's legs began to turn blue.

Immediately upon arrival, Mutti was carried in and the delivery continued. The doctor was able to birth the rest of the baby, though the umbilical cord was wrapped around her neck and ear. Making a spectacular entry into the world, my baby sister arrived in the early morning hours of November 15, 1948, healthy and fit. Even though my mother had planned to name the baby Rebecca if it was a girl, for some reason she changed her mind at the last minute. My sister was named Ruth. Prince Charles of England was born a few hours earlier, shortly before midnight of November 14th. England had won again!

Papa stayed over night in Munich with my mother. At school the following day, I excitedly told my classmates about my new sister. Then, during our first period, my friend Franz decided to announce the arrival of my sister to the rest of the class during our equivalent of "Show and Tell." He stood up and excitedly announced, "Erika had a little baby!" Everyone burst out laughing and Franz realized he had meant to say, "Erika had a little sister." He turned bright red with embarrassment. Even strict Mr. Bierling burst out laughing!

Above, Papa, my little sister Ruth, and me

Two-year-old Ruth with me in 1950

20 ~ A New Life

With the arrival of Ruth, our family seemed complete. Our tenants downstairs, the Blum family, finally moved out. Papa hoped to keep the whole house for our own family now, but the housing shortage made it mandatory for us to lease to another family. Our next tenants, a middle-aged couple with an older son and ten-year-old daughter, only stayed one year. Then we had the whole house to ourselves at last. We also had a new bathroom installed with running water. We were now facing a new chapter in our lives. Life was good again.

After turning fourteen in December, I was looking forward to finishing elementary school in a few short months. Following elementary school, girls typically learned a trade and attended business school simultaneously. Jobs were very scarce in this postwar period. I was grateful to my teacher, Mr. Bierling, for recommending a position for me with a friend of his who owned a radio/electric store. This store would later be the first in our town to sell television sets. Mr. Bierling told his friend I would be excellent at accounting and selling. The owner, Herr B., had a position open and offered me the job. I received special permission from my school principal to leave school several weeks before graduation in order to accept the position. I was so grateful to have a job at such a young age and in such a depressed economy.

My new job was in Fuerstenfeldbruck, about one mile away from Emmering. At first, I walked to work. Later, I had a bicycle and rode to work, or caught the bus. There were 2 different ways to get to work. One was the scenic route: walking through the woods and crossing over bridges along the Amper River, and passing by a pond filled with geese and ducks. The other way was the fast way: walking through town, watching out for cars and bicycles and pedestrians, grateful for the policemen directing traf-

Fuerstenfeldbruck

fic. I preferred the scenic route but sometimes had to choose the faster way if I wanted to be on time to my job.

My first day on the job was overwhelming. My boss, Herr B., introduced me to his wife, a very kind lady who looked to be in her mid-forties. Herr B. was in his early fifties. My boss and his wife had three children: a son and two daughters. I was also introduced to Miss Anni, a friend of the family who took care of the children part-time. She conveniently lived across the street. I also met Lotte, the full-time maid. The family lived in a large apartment located above the store.

My first job was at a radio-electric store in Fuerstenfeldbruck

After meeting the household, Herr B. introduced me to the employees in the warehouse. They were responsible to repair any electric appliance, large or small. The technicians repaired radios and, as they became more available, televisions. They also handled electric installations in new and remodeled homes.

I was hired to handle the accounting, selling, and repairing minor electric appliances. I also was responsible to keep everything clean in the showroom. This meant lots of dusting on a daily basis and cleaning the large showroom windows. I worked from 8:00 in the morning until noon, and then again from 2:00 in the afternoon until 6:00 in the evening. On Wednesday, the store closed at noon. On that day, I went to business school all day long. On Saturdays, I worked from 8:00 in the morning until 4:00 in the afternoon. I was usually off on Sundays. If I walked home for lunch, I generally covered about five miles a day between home and work.

I did not exactly love my job. However, being an apprentice was not expected to be a great experience. My monthly paycheck only amounted to about six dollars for the first year, nine dollars the second year, and eleven dollars my third year. Part of every paycheck went to my mother for room and board. Everyone who worked gave a portion to their family. That was the expected thing to do. After all, Mutti bought my clothing and provided for other necessities. I still had money left over to use as I pleased. I looked forward to the time when my apprenticeship would end. After three years, I would graduate from business school and complete "meine Lehre."

As time went on, my job became more and more routine. I learned a lot about accounting, and combined with what I was learning at business school, I felt very accomplished. I even enjoyed selling small electric appliances and handling minor repair work for the business. However, dusting the showroom every day was not my favorite job responsibility. I also felt uneasy around my boss, Herr B. I noticed that he looked at me frequently, and sometimes made inappropriate comments. I learned from some of the other employees that Herr B. had an affair with a previous employee which broke up his marriage. Though his wife still lived in the same home with him, they had separate bedrooms now. Frau B. stayed only to help run the business.

Frau B. was a very nice lady who always dressed professionally. I always felt better when she came downstairs to help in the office and did part of the selling. Being alone with my boss was scary. Sometimes he could not keep his hands to himself and I had to push him away. He was an ugly middle-aged man. I was a young innocent teenager and had no interest in someone of his age. I frequently couldn't wait until work was over so I could meet with friends my own age.

Often, I met friends on Sundays after church was over and dinner was finished. Margit had accepted a job at the courthouse as an apprentice. I frequently spent time with her until she finished business school and moved to Munich. We would walk to the next town of Fuerstenfeldbruck to see a movie or just go for walks. During this time, I met a girl named Sigrid who was six months younger than me.

My friend Margit

Like Margit, Sigrid had come to Bavaria as part of the wave of refugees from the east zone at the end of the war. Sigrid's parents had adopted her—she never knew what happened to her real parents, or if they were dead or alive. Sometimes the war simply took away parents or children, and others stepped in to fill the void. Her adoptive parents and brother were very loving towards her and treated her like she was their own.

Sigrid worked for a well known fur dealership in Fuerstenfeldbruck. We had a lot in common and Sigrid became my best friend. We did everything together. Sigrid was not very happy with her position at the fur store, so when an opening at my location became available, I recommended her for the position. She began working for Herr B. as

My friend Sigrid came to work at the store with me

well. This made work so much more enjoyable, particularly since Sigrid took over the dusting and cleaning! Sigrid and I had a blast whenever Herr B. was not around. Soon we began double-dating on Sundays and sharing all our secrets with each other.

On special occasions we German girls were invited to the new youth center sponsored by the American Officers Wives Club at Fuerstenfeldbruck Air Base. One of my friends and I decided to go. That night was B I N G O Night. It did not take very long until I figured out what Bingo was and how to play it. I guess it was beginner's luck, but I won a very nice winter coat. I desperately needed one too. What was really nice is that it was exactly my size. Mutti was all excited. Now she didn't have to spend money on me for a coat. We did not have a lot especially after my sister Ruth was born. If someone received something new, it was my baby sister. She always came first.

When Germany's annual festival of Fasching came along, my boss paid for another employee and myself to take dancing lessons. Fasching is a very big deal in Germany. Invitations were sent to businesses. Normally the owner and his wife would attend. But sometimes there was more than one invitation sent for the same day but in different cafes or restaurants; when this occurred, the company was represented by two of their chosen employees. Herr B. wanted his business represented well, and chose me to be one of the company's representatives. He also chose Friedoline (Friedl for short), one of our outstanding apprenticeship mechanics. He sent us both to take six weeks' worth of dancing lessons.

On the night of the big event, Friedl and I went to the Brameshuber Café, one of the better class places in town for lots of music and dancing. A large guestroom was reserved for this special occasion. Friedl and I met at the café. He looked very sharp in his traditional Bavarian outfit. This was my first time to go out by myself with a co-worker at night. We were seated at a corner table and served a glass of wine. At first, it felt a little uneasy to start a conversation and we simply listened to the music. After a while, Friedl warmed up a bit, and spoke about his favorite activities, like riding his bike with friends to the nearby mountains. He also loved mountain-climbing. After a delicious meal, the dance floor was open. Friedl was a little shy but did ask me to dance and we had a great time.

Friedl loved mountain-climbing more than dancing

That evening was so much fun for me that I wanted to be able to go out more often. My mother gave me permission to go to local dances in Emmering or Fuerstenfeldbruck, like spring festivals and the summer fest. Usually my parents attended as well. As time went on I began dating, though I had no serious or steady relationships until much later.

Sigrid and I went out every weekend, meeting other friends who joined us. We would walk for hours up and down the market place in our high heels. Most of the young people hung out at the marketplace. One day, I met a very nice looking man named Franz at the summer festival. He had pretty dark brown wavy hair and brown eyes. He wore a brown leather jacket and drove a BMW motorcycle which he kept shiny clean. It seemed like all eyes were on him and his BMW.

Sigrid and I enjoyed spending all our free time together

Franz came from Munich about seventeen miles away from Emmering. He was a couple of years older then I was. I loved his pretty smile and his southern accent. We never had a set date and we had no phone to stay in contact. But I listened for the sound of his BMW outside our front door; he generally appeared on weekends or after work. Franz and I saw each other quite regularly, and cruised around all over Emmering and Fuerstenfeldbruck. My friends envied me because of his good looks and motorcycle.

By now, I was seventeen years old now and had graduated from business school. I received my diploma as a "Kaufmannische Angestellte" in Accounting and Minor Electrical Repairs. This meant I received a promotion and large pay increase at my job. Things were looking good.

On my eighteenth birthday, Sigrid gave me a red leather diary. I made a few entries but unfortunately did not keep up with it. After living a lifetime's worth of excitement and despair, tragedy and drama, in the span of a few years, I couldn't come up with anything worthwhile to write. The war was over. My father and brother were gone. I had a new home, a new father, and new sister, and a bright new life.

The past began to fade from my memory like old photographs exposed to the sunlight—faded, but not forgotten, waiting for the day when the people from the past would demand to be remembered.

Epilog

Looking back over those first eighteen years of my life, I see not just the hard times during the war, though those memories are forever imprinted in my mind. I also see the good things, the friendships, the laughter, the moments when life was kind and people loving. Though the loss of my father and my brother cannot be erased, others have come into my life and given me warm relationships and happy memories. Life can be hard, but life can also be rewarding. Perhaps we all must take the bad with the good and make the most of the opportunities God gives us, being grateful for the moments when all is right with the world, even if it is only for a moment.

My relationship with Franz didn't last forever. Over the ensuring years, I dated other men until I found the one I would spend the rest of my life with. After eight years of working for the Electric and Radio Company, I found a better paying job in Ramstein, Germany. After moving there, I met an American G.I. named Jim Zeigler, stationed at Ramstein Air

Base. He became the final man with dark wavy hair and brown eyes that would sweep me off my feet. In 1960, I became an Air Force wife. After two years, we moved from Germany to Williams Air Force Base in Arizona. By then, we had two daughters with a third on the way.

As an Air Force family with three daughters, we moved frequently. In 1966, my husband was transferred to Morocco on the northwest coast of Africa on special assignment as an advisor to the Moroccan Air Force. The whole family packed up and moved for a one year stay in Kenitra, near Rabat, the capital of Morocco. When our time in Africa was over, I was very glad to learn we were being transferred to Wiesbaden, Germany for another year and a half. It was good to visit friends and family again.

After Germany, we moved back to the states. Jim accepted an assignment to Carswell Air Force Base in Ft. Worth, Texas. I began working part-time on base and at Montgomery Ward store while our children went to school. During that time, Jim was given a six month assignment in Okinawa, and a one-year assignment in Thailand; both trips were assigned as temporary duty which meant he could not take his family. The girls and I stayed at Carswell while Jim finished both assignments overseas.

After he returned, we accompanied him to what would be our last transfer to Griffiss Air Force Base in New York. By now our daughters were in junior high and high school. During our two and a half years in New York, I again worked on base for Civilian Personnel. Finally, in 1975, after twenty-one years in the Air Force, Jim retired and brought the family back to Fort Worth to live permanently. He took a job with the Xerox Corporation in Fort Worth and retired a second time after putting in twenty-two years. I also worked in Fort Worth at the Levitz Furniture store, retiring after twenty years.

Over the years, I have visited Germany and my friends and family often, and lived to see many of them pass away. Frau Dudek, our friendly neighbor who took me to see my new baby brother after he was born, passed away in the mid-1960s. I had lost touch with her many years earlier. My dear friend Sigrid married and had two daughters and a son. She divorced early on and remarried a very nice man named Heinz. They live happily in Munich, Germany.

On my father's side of the family, Opa Bredt died at the age of eighty-four after a long illness. Oma

Bredt suffered a head injury at the age of eighty-five when she was hit by a car while crossing the street. She never fully recovered from her injury and passed away six months later.

Shortly after the war ended, Tante Martha divorced her husband when he left her for a much younger woman. She remarried much later in life to Heinrich, a long-time friend of the family. Their marriage lasted seventeen years until he passed away in 1991 at the age of eighty-nine. Tante Martha lived the next fourteen years alone. The last year of her life she suffered a stroke that paralyzed her, leaving her unable to speak. She died in January 2005 at the age of ninety-six.

Tante Martha's daughters, Edith and Renate have both passed away as well. My cousin Renate died of colon cancer at the age of sixty-six in September of 1997. I lost touch with Edith, Tante Martha's other daughter. She was married to a man named Erich; they had a daughter and a son. Erich died at the early age of forty of a brain tumor. Much later, I learned she became an alcoholic. She died in January 2009 in Moenchengladbach, Germany.

On my mother's side of the family, my grandmother Boeckem passed away at age sixty-six of a stroke. Grandpa Boeckem lived to be eighty-nine. That same week Tante Martha passed away, my Tante Gertrud, Mutti's younger sister also passed away at age eighty-seven. Her husband Hans passed away in the 1980s. Tante Gertrud had three children—two sons and one daughter. Hans-Josef, the second son, died unexpectedly of a heart attack at age forty. His older brother Ingo and wife Ingrid have one daughter and a grandson named Nick. They currently live in Fuldathal, Germany. Ingo's sister Ursula is single and lives with her boyfriend Meinhard in Moenchengladbach, Germany.

After the war ended, Mutti's brother Josef married a girl named Maria and had two sons. He died at the age of seventy-seven in February of 1997. Berti married twice and had five children. He suffered a stroke and lived for a time in a nursing home in Moenchengladbach, Germany. He passed away on May 6, 2009, as I was completing this book.

Mutti found out she had esophageal cancer in 1988. She went into the hospital on her seventy-third birthday in preparation for major surgery on her stomach and esophagus. One week after the surgery, her organs failed one by one. She died in April of 1988. I was in the States during her surgery, fully expecting to receive news from my sister Ruth that the operation was successful. I was shocked and terribly saddened by the passing of my mother. My stepfather Karl passed away eleven years later, five days short of his ninetieth birthday. My sister Ruth was married twice and divorced twice. She recently retired from many years working for the German postal service. She lives near Munich with her live-in boyfriend Wolfgang. She never had any children.

The Zeigler Family

As for me, I currently live in Fort Worth, Texas with my husband Jim. Both of us are doing well and enjoy spending time with our three daughters and their husbands, five grandchildren, and one great-grandson. After forty-nine years of marriage, I can gratefully say that my life has been full of love.

Made in the USA